INTRODUCTION

Eddie was the kind of man who gave his all to his job. He worked hard night and day, and as a parent he felt he should encourage his children to work just as hard. His "contribution" to his children was made up of motivational statements. "You can do it. You can make the team," he'd say. "Do your best. Get out there and win." For Eddie believed that your value as a person was defined by what you could do well in life.

It didn't take long for Eddie's wife, Ilene, to feel that she had to perform outside the home in order to feel good about herself. So, even though she had always felt the most valuable thing she could do was be a wife and mother, she was drawn out of the home and into a career.

The children too began to look outside the home for personal worth and value. They joined teams. They played in the school band. They took part-time jobs. Under Eddie's well-intentioned leadership, family time together became nonexistent. If the family actually sat down at the dinner table together, it was only to nourish their bodies before each one ran out into the world to perform.

Then one day the worst possible thing happened to Eddie. The nurturer of his self-esteem, the company that had rewarded his hard work with promotions, closed its doors. He was out of work.

Eddie was not only out of a job—he was in shock. Without an arena to perform in, Eddie felt worthless. How could he tell his family he was out of work? How could they love him when he had failed? Just when he needed unconditional love and acceptance the most, he had no idea how to get it. Out of work to Eddie meant that he didn't deserve to be loved.

To his surprise, rather than rejecting him, Eddie's family rallied around him. For the first time Eddie realized that his self-esteem could come from belonging to a family who loved him regardless of how he performed. He saw how pushing for performance had driven his family away from each other, and he began the long process of drawing his family together, encouraging them to find happiness and purpose in their unconditional love for each other. Eventually Eddie, Ilene, and the children enjoyed a relationship more wonderful than they had ever thought possible.

We all have something of Eddie in us. We all grew up believing that a person's value is determined by performance. And we pass on that very same belief to our children, conditioning them to search for their identity and their value by looking out in the world. By doing so, we parents chase the children out of the home and away from the much-needed, nurturing family relationship.

If we are to raise confident kids—kids who feel good about themselves—they should not feel as if they have to leave home to find personal worth. Home is where they should feel the most valuable—not for what they can do or how well they can perform, but for who they are: our children.

Raising Confident Kids

Raising
Confident
Kids

Previously published as
Confident Kids

ROBERT G. BARNES, JR.

ZondervanPublishingHouse
Grand Rapids, Michigan

A Division of HarperCollinsPublishers

RAISING CONFIDENT KIDS
Copyright © 1992 by Robert G. Barnes, Jr.

Requests for information should be addressed to:
Zondervan Publishing House
Grand Rapids, Michigan 49530

Library of Congress Cataloging-in-Publication Data

Barnes, Robert G., 1947–
    Raising confident kids / Robert G. Barnes, Jr.
      p. cm.
    Originally published under title: Confident kids.
    ISBN 0-310-54511-0 (pbk.)
    1. Parenting—United States. 2. Self-respect in children.
    3. Parenting—Religious aspects—Christianity. I. Barnes, Robert
    G., 1947– Confident kids. II. Title.
    HQ755.85.B3637   1992
    649'.1—dc20   91–34792
                                        CIP

The pronouns he/him and she/her are frequently used generically and
interchangeably in this book.

Edited by Lori J. Walburg
Cover designed by David Marty

Printed in the United States of America

92 93 94 95 96 97 / AM / 10 9 8 7 6 5 4 3 2 1

CONTENTS

PART IV What Else Do I Need to Teach My Child?

PART V How Do I Handle My Teenager?

PART I

What Is
Self-Esteem?

1

SELF-ESTEEM BEGINS AT HOME

When Torrey, my oldest child, went off to school at five years old, something very strange took place. Up to this point in Torrey's life, Mom and Dad had been her key fans, sitting in the bleachers, applauding her accomplishments. We had taught her to look to her parents for love and praise. As a result, she was a happy, confident child.

Torrey herself did not change when she started school. She continued to come to us with her latest paper from school or with the playground stories of the day. But *I* changed my response to her.

For some reason that I cannot explain, when Torrey began school, I felt that she did not need my approval as much as before. She was older now and other people, such as her teacher, were in charge. I still looked at her papers with her, but I began to miss some key events in her life.

A Grave Error

One day Torrey announced that her kindergarten class was putting on a play the next Tuesday evening. Naturally, she assumed we would be there. But I said, "That's a busy night for me, Torrey. I'll try to be there, but I may have to meet with some families that night."

Torrey looked at me, bewildered. She had never thought that her daddy might not come to the play. I had always been in the cheering section before. Why would I not be there now? She walked away hurt and confused. I passed it off as a part of growing up and assured myself that she would get over it.

Not long after that event, I was walking in my neighborhood when I heard shouts and yells coming from the YMCA. It was a soccer game, a contest between two teams of six-year-olds. Thirty boys dressed in red and blue scrambled madly for the ball while their coaches shouted and the referee made calls and blew the whistle.

As I sat on the lawn enjoying the game, I glanced around and noticed that I was in a minority. Out of thirty children, only four parents had taken the time out to watch their child.

As I watched the coaches gesture and call, I realized that the parents had turned their children over to a coach as a substitute parent. So I watched the coaches' performance as a parent. I looked for individual attention, for evidences of unconditional love.

I saw neither. The coaches gave the most attention to the boys with the most ability. The other boys either stood around the coach, trying to get his attention, or had given up altogether and were at the far end of the field wrestling, laughing, and giving each other the attention they needed. The coaches, who are performance oriented, had to focus on the performance of the child playing. They had no time for the children on the bench.

I thought about those absent parents picking up their sons after the game and trying to have a meaningful conversation. Both parent and son would have a difficult time discussing the event. The parents would not know enough about what went on to ask questions that required more than one-word answers.

PARENT: Well, how was the big game?
CHILD: Fine.
PARENT: Did you win?
CHILD: Yes.
PARENT: Did you get into the game?
CHILD: Yes.
PARENT: Well, how did you do?
CHILD: Fine.
PARENT: Well, that's great. We need to get right home so that you can get your bath and dinner before the baby-sitter arrives.

They may have a better conversation if the boy scored a goal or made some spectacular play. However, a conversation like this focuses only on performance. The whole afternoon, the boy's relationship both with the coach and with his chauffeur/parent was based on his abilities rather than on his value as a person.

I walked away from that afternoon soccer game saddened and very judgmental. To show the children they were valuable, the parents should have attended and shown an interest in the game and the child no matter how well the child played.

On the way back home, however, it hit me. I was guilty of the very same thing. I had raised Torrey for the first five years to believe that she was very valuable and important to me. I had watched her take her first steps and tackle other new feats, and she always knew we were applauding *her*, not her performance. Then one day, she began school, and instead of being there for her as I had always been, for some reason I pulled back. No wonder she was bewildered.

"Subcontracting" the Job of Raising Self-Esteem

When building a house, a general contractor is in charge of the whole project. Often, however, he will hire other professionals, such as carpenters or plumbers, to do part of the job for him.

We already learned from Eddie's story that self-image comes not from performance, but from relationships, especially family relationships. But parents, as the "general contractors" of the child's self-esteem, have somehow been led to believe that they can do only a very minor part of the job. So they "subcontract" their children out to coaches and teachers and instructors.

Take Darlene as an example. Darlene is a mother of two children, Joey, eight years old, and Brenda, six years old. Convinced that children need a mother's nurturing, she and her husband decided that she would be a full-time mother.

As the children grew older, Darlene felt they needed to be involved in activities outside the home. So Darlene began to shuttle her children back and forth from the activities that would build their self-esteem. Mondays and Thursdays were gymnastic lessons. Tuesdays were Joey's trumpet lesson, Wednesday was children's choir practice, and Saturday was Brenda's piano lessons.

Darlene had placed her children in excellent activities. Each skill they learned would certainly help them perform better. Darlene did exactly what the "super mom" is supposed to do.

One day, however, she noticed that her children were becoming more and more distant from her. Though they spent hours in the car together, the children no longer looked to her for encouragement and opinions. In fact, they didn't even bother to tell her stories anymore.

Darlene realized that she had demoted herself. She had gone from being a full-time mom who actively involved herself in her children's lives to being a mere chauffeur. In her quest to help Joey and Brenda develop a positive self-image, she had "subcontracted the job" out, turning her children over to someone else and, in the process, abdicating her role as mother to become a chauffeur.

Darlene is not alone in this mistake. Many parents pile on more and more skills to their child's repertoire, not realizing that healthy self-esteem does not develop from skills acquired outside the home. Rather, a good self-image is nurtured at home.

That is not to say that outside activities are bad; in fact, they can be very valuable. The crime occurs when parents push children from one event to the next without getting involved. Our children have come to expect that we will be in their cheering section, and if we leave those seats of encouragement empty, something else will quickly take our place.

That "something else" is their peers. Today's child spends more time with his peers than his parents—and for good reason. If Mom and Dad aren't sitting in the cheering section, a child will change his performances and antics to please his peers. We parents can actually force our children to look outside the family for approval. But a child's peers will never, *never* be able to give her the valuable feedback she needs to develop a positive self-concept. The peer himself is too needy in this area to have much to hand out.

Fortunately for Darlene and her family, she caught her mistake in time and made the necessary changes, cutting back on outside activities. And fortunately for Torrey, I too realized where I had failed her. And I quickly returned to my old seat in her "cheering section."

2

LEARNING TO VALUE YOURSELF

Like all of us parents, Darlene wanted her children to be confident and happy. She knew her children needed a healthy self-image; she just chose the wrong means to reach a good end. Perhaps if she had stopped for a minute to think about self-image, she would have had a better idea of how to develop it in her children.

The problem boils down to definition. Just what is this thing called self-esteem?

People have always asked themselves, "Who am I? Am I OK?" In the quest to "find themselves," they have traveled, taken various jobs, gone to college, read books, or married, always hoping that one of these things would give them identity and self-worth.

Self-esteem is how you value yourself. You try to answer the question "Who am I?" by saying "I am valuable." But you cannot evaluate that value only by looking at yourself. Nor can outside things alone—whether they be a job, a marriage partner, or a college degree—build your self-esteem. Instead, you form your self-esteem by evaluating the way other significant people view you.

One of my friends, Joel Lampart, is an artist. Joel often goes to weekend art shows to display his paintings. He sits near his booth not to look at his work, but to observe the way people react and respond to it. If he has initially priced one of his paintings at $500 and no one responds to it, after a while he assumes that the painting must be less valuable than he thought, so he lowers the price.

Joel sometimes finds it difficult to sit there while people discuss his work. "Those paintings are pieces of myself," he told me, "and sometimes they don't like what they see. But I need to hear their comments in order to judge how well I am doing."

Our self-esteem is closely tied to who we think we are. And we usually decide our value by looking at the way others see us and value us. Just as Joel decided the value of his paintings by the responses he observed, so we decide our value by how others react to us.

A Mirror Image

People's responses to us reflect our image back to us like a mirror. We need mirrors to help us find out how we appear. I once read of a man kept in solitary confinement for two years. One of the things he missed was a mirror. He kept asking the guards, "How do I look?"

The significant people around us—family, friends, and co-workers—act as mirrors. The way they reflect back at us, or respond to us, tells us who we are and how valuable we are. In a sense, we each ask the "mirrors" around us the same question the prisoner asked, "How do I look?"

Often, however, the people around us don't reflect an accurate image. Remember standing in front of those fun-house mirrors? One mirror stretched you out till you were bean-pole thin. Another made you look like the Pillsbury dough boy.

People are like those fun-house mirrors. Shaped by their own personal needs and difficulties, they often aren't capable of reflecting back a true image. Even parents, because of emotional difficulties, sometimes cannot reflect a true image to their child. The child will leave this "warped mirror" feeling unloved and worthless.

Lisa's parents are a classic example of the damage a warped mirror can do to a child's self-image. When she was a child, her parents told her over and over that she was fat. They led her to believe that "to be valuable you must lose weight" or "to gain my approval you must not be overweight." Soon Lisa thought that her only identifying characteristic was her weight.

As Lisa grew, she slimmed down naturally. At twenty she was trim and beautiful, and many friends, male and female, complimented her on her fitness. Yet she still thought of herself as fat, and secretly she began to drastically cut back on her food intake. Because the mirror of her life had continually ridiculed her for being overweight, Lisa eventually developed anorexia nervosa and nearly starved herself to death.

We never develop our self-esteem objectively. Lisa probably was not conscious of the fact that she was trying to receive parental approval and self-esteem through controlling her weight. Instead, we gain our self-esteem through a very subjective, unconscious process of trying to perceive and evaluate how other people see us.

Lisa received the label "fat." Other children are stuck with the label "bad." Parents will say, "Nathan, how can you be so bad?" rather than, "Nathan, you have done a very bad thing." Children need to know that it is the behavior that is bad, not themselves.

Children also need to know that they can be forgiven for bad behavior. By forgiving children you help them erase the warp in their self-esteem mirror. Then they can safely return to the mirror (their parents) for more reflections. Instead of seeing themselves as "bad," they will learn to see certain behaviors as bad. And they will learn that even if they make bad choices, forgiveness can clean the slate and give them an opportunity to make better choices.

Peer Reflections

Although parents play an important part in our quest for self-esteem, peers are also important. I grew up in a small city on Long Island and went through elementary and junior high school with the same peers. Over the years I had learned how to read their reflections, and I knew whose opinions I valued. In Long Island my self-esteem was strong because I knew my friends valued me. However, in high school my family moved from Long Island to a suburb of Washington, D.C., and I soon learned that all those years of positive reflections did not cast my self-esteem in stone.

Bethesda, Maryland had a new, strong, and very definite social structure. The teenagers dressed differently, talked differently, and followed different social models than I did. The boys wore their hair in a short "Princeton cut," while my hair was long and "early Elvis," like the rest of Long Island. Everywhere I looked, the new mirrors reflected back to me that I was different and unacceptable.

Unable to deal with these new mirrors, I changed abruptly. Whereas in Long Island I had participated in sports, band, and student council, in Bethesda I dropped out of band, attempted only one sport, and certainly did not run for any offices. I soon felt so worthless that I became a chronic truant. I just could not handle the new reflections I was receiving.

Daily Evaluation

The quest for self-esteem has no end. It is not something you attain once in life and then feel valuable forever after. Self-esteem is an ongoing process, a daily evaluation.

In the Old Testament, when Elijah encountered the prophets of Baal, he knew who he was. He measured his self-esteem by his relationship to God. He was so secure in his self-esteem that he stood there alone, taunting the 450 pagan priests as they called on their gods. The confidence he demonstrated in his verbal jabs was amazing.

"At noon Elijah began to taunt them. 'Shout louder!' he said. 'Surely he is a god! Perhaps he is deep in thought, or busy, or traveling. Maybe he is sleeping and must be awakened'" (1 Kings 18:27).

Elijah went on to win that contest and was so elated that later on that day he ran back to town faster than the king's chariots. At that moment he knew who he was—a powerful prophet of God.

Yet already in the next chapter Elijah is a broken man, fleeing for his life and begging the Lord to allow him to die. How quickly his self-esteem was dashed! No matter how great and decisive the victory God had given him, at that moment Elijah felt that life was no longer worth living.

A Reason for Living

During the late 1930s and early 1940s, millions of people, Jews and Gentiles, were murdered in concentration camps—one of the worst atrocities the world has ever known. Victor Frankl, a psychiatrist and prisoner in one of the camps, reported another more subtle form of murder that took place in the camps—the murder of the prisoners' value as persons.

Because of his medical background, Frankl worked in the infirmary, where he saw and talked with many of the prisoners. He saw prisoners tortured, raped, experimented on as if they were animals, and finally, gassed for no reason. He saw prisoners degraded to the point that they felt they were of no value to anyone, not even themselves.

In early December 1944, word spread through the camp that the Allied forces were coming. All the prisoners would be freed before Christmas! Suddenly the whole mood of the prison camp changed. Even though the December cold was fierce, admissions to the infirmary dwindled. Prisoners once again began to feel they were valuable—valuable enough for the Allied forces to fight mile by mile to free.

Christmas and New Year's Day passed with no Allied troops in sight. The week after New Year's Day, the infirmary filled up, and hundreds of prisoners died—not in executions this time, but from "natural causes." When the Allies failed to come at the "appointed" time, people felt more worthless than ever. Their self-esteem totally destroyed, great numbers of the prisoners simply lay down and died.

Self-esteem can be a reason for living. Some prisoners, like Frankl, refused to accept the way they were treated as an appraisal of their personal value. Others, however, had been stripped of all self-esteem and, like Elijah, lost their will to live.

We never, once and for all, establish our self-esteem. New reflections from significant others will continue to have an impact on our evaluations of who we are and how much we are worth.

3

FINDING A PLACE TO BELONG

All of us need to belong to something or someone. Take Ellen, for example. Although she was only six years old, she had been so abused and neglected by her mother that she could not figure out why she was being treated so badly. Finally she asked her mother, "Do I belong to you, Mommy?"

An older woman, Elizabeth, also demonstrated that innate need to belong. When she was asked for a brief biography to be read before her keynote speech, Elizabeth gave her name, education, family situation, church home, club memberships, and more—all to prove to the audience that she "belonged."

People do not evaluate who they are or how valuable they are by isolating themselves from others. In fact, the opposite is true. We evaluate our worth by the way we connect with or belong to other groups. Belonging to something—a family, team, company, or group of people—is vital to our self-esteem and helps us to complete a basic part of the puzzle of who we are.

On the surface, at least, we all "belong" to various groups. More important to our self-esteem, however, is how we perceive our place in those groups. Are we a valuable member of these groups? Do we feel indispensable? If not, our self-esteem may suffer.

Everyone Must Find a Place to Belong

As a junior in college I was president of my fraternity. Although the relationships within the fraternity were mostly superficial, I felt that I was a valuable member of the group and that they needed me. My fraternity brothers' approval of me validated my worth.

That all changed, however, when I gave my life to Christ. I began to distance myself from the questionable activities of the fraternity. I no longer partied every weekend. I cleaned up my language and made other changes in my lifestyle that distanced me from the fraternity. As a result, the fraternity gave me less and less approval.

For a time I stayed in the fraternity, trying to ignore their disapproval. But I couldn't. For two years the group had reinforced my value as a person. Now, under their disapproving gaze, I felt almost worthless. Although I was doing well academically, I was so depressed by their rejection that I nearly quit college. I knew I needed to belong somewhere, but I saw no alternatives. My choice seemed clear: belong to Christ and quit school, or belong to the fraternity and graduate.

One night, in the midst of this inner turmoil, I was invited to a campus Bible study. I had never been to one before and probably would not have gone had I not been feeling lonely and confused. As it was, I nearly didn't stay when I arrived late to find the room already filled with about twenty students, most of whom I barely knew.

The room got quiet as I walked in. *Oh, no,* I thought, *I don't belong here. Why did I even come?* Just when I felt I couldn't stand their gaze any longer, the young man leading the study stood up and said, "Come on in and sit down, Bob. We've got a seat for you right over here."

I almost said, "Who, me?" I even wanted to turn around and make sure that there wasn't another Bob standing behind me. Trying to hide my nervousness, I walked over and sat down in the seat next to the leader. He spotted my brand-new Bible, reached for it, and commented about how nice it was. When he handed it back, it was opened to the chapter and verse that they were studying, and I was saved the embarrassment of having to ask, "How do I find Ephesians?"

The study lasted for an hour. Afterwards, the leader said, "It was good to have you here, Bob. I hope you'll be back next week." I did not yet feel completely comfortable with this new group. But that week various members of the Bible study group went out of their way to approach me and make me feel special.

I went to the Bible study the next week and many weeks afterward. It was a major transition in my life. As I was feeling less and less like I belonged or was valuable to my fraternity, I was feeling more and more like I belonged to this new group that made me feel special from the very beginning.

Slowly I transferred my allegiance from the fraternity to the Christian community. To be sure, I didn't immediately become a leader in the group. I needed to feel secure in my own identity before I could reach out to others. Finally, however, I was secure enough that I began my own Bible study—quite a step up in my new self-image. I had found a place where I belonged.

Belonging Allows Us to Feel Needed

To feel the sense of belonging, we need to establish relationships. Those relationships not only help us feel valuable, but they also give us the confidence we need to contribute to the welfare of others. And having the opportunity to contribute is extremely important to one's self-esteem.

Our contributions are two-pronged. First, we contribute toward the welfare of the group that we belong to. Second, as a part of a group, we contribute to society in general. To feel secure in any group, we need to feel good not only about the group itself, but also about the group's mission.

Since 1974 I have worked at Sheridan House Family Ministries, a residential treatment center for teenage boys and girls. Years ago, an elderly lady called Sheridan House to ask for help. The grapefruit trees in her backyard were loaded with fruit and she desperately needed someone to pick the grapefruit for her.

I walked into one of the boys' homes asking for volunteers. Not one volunteered. Deciding to put a bit more excitement into my voice, I went to another boys' home. Finally, I got some reluctant volunteers.

All morning we worked picking grapefruit. It was back-breaking work, and by the time we finished we were all hot, itchy, and sweaty. We sprawled out on the lawn to catch our breath before heading back to the home.

Just then the elderly woman came out, lemonade in hand and a smile of gratitude on her face. As she served us lemonade and thanked us—the only way she could afford to pay us—the boys' tired faces began to light up. As exhausted as they were, the boys felt great. For the first time in their lives, they belonged to a group that had contributed to the welfare of someone in need.

The experience made such an impression on the boys that I was the only one to groan when one of the boys shouted as we drove off, "Call us again; we'll come back and help." Watching the reaction of these normally sullen boys, I realized how important it is to belong to a group where members feel needed.

The family, too, should be a special group where children feel that they belong and are needed. When the family helps everyone feel valuable and needed, children will have better self-esteem. This doesn't happen when the family spends its time dropping the children off elsewhere. In fact, this only hinders the family from learning to function as a unit.

If you want to learn what it really means to function as a unit, take your family camping. Outdoors, everyone in the family is needed—to gather wood, to set up the tent, to start a fire. And the finished product of everyone working together—the campsite—is easy to see.

What's a Group Worth?

The way we view the groups to which we belong can also affect our self-esteem. In other words, not only do we need to belong to a group, we also need the group itself to be worthwhile.

For example, in the post-Vietnam War era, our self-esteem as a nation plummeted. Reeling from the disillusionment of Watergate and the devastation of the war, we no longer took pride in being part of the large group—the United States. And our self-esteem, even as individuals, suffered.

If something as large and impersonal as a nation can affect our individual self-esteem, one can only imagine the effect of a poorly functioning family on a child's self-esteem. However, a family does not achieve its worth by winning wars or achieving economic prosperity, as nations do. Nor should a family pursue worth through faulty means, such as accomplishments, possessions, personality, or beauty. None of these things ultimately make a family valuable. Rather, a family's worth is determined by the amount of love it conveys.

God created us with a need to belong, and it is through belonging to a family that each member—son, daughter, mother, and father—nurtures his or her self-esteem. It is crucial to our self-esteem to belong to a loving family, one that will value us regardless of how we perform. The remainder of this book will show you how to create a loving atmosphere to nurture self-esteem in your family members.

4

THE FAMILY: GOD'S MECHANISM
FOR SELF-ESTEEM

God created the family to offer, as no other group on earth could, unconditional love to each of its members. In the family, each member sees value in the other members— value for *who* they are rather than for *what they can do*.

If you question this understanding of the family, analyze the family dynamics in one of Jesus' best-known parables.

Once there was a boy who didn't feel very good about himself. He had a loving family: his father was a prosperous farmer, and his older brother a hard worker. Yet this boy didn't feel rich enough, famous enough, successful enough by that day's standards. Quite frankly, he wanted more from life. He wanted money.

So the boy went to his father, palm out, and asked for his inheritance. He didn't want to have to wait till his father died. He wanted it *now*. His father scratched at his beard thoughtfully. "All right," he finally said. "You may have it." And he promptly divided his property and gave the younger son his share of the estate.

As if the boy's request weren't rude enough, the boy heaped insult onto injury. He took the money and headed out to a distant country to squander his wealth in wild living. To make himself into a "somebody," this ungrateful child took what his father had worked many years to gain—and sold it. How he must have broken his father's heart!

But the boy didn't think about that. He had beautiful women hanging on his arm, and lots of buddies to party with. What a boost to his self-esteem! Finally, he was "somebody" in the eyes of the world.

Little by little, however, his money slowly leaked away. With it went his friends. Even his ability to survive was in danger. Abandoned by his friends, bereft of any money, he took the only job available: feeding pigs. His Jewish background forbade him to eat pork, let alone raise it, but he had nowhere else to turn. He had hit rock bottom.

One day, however, the boy came to his senses. *Hey,* he thought, *even my father's workers are treated better than I am here. I'm going home.*

Meanwhile, back home on the family farm, the boy's father had not given up hope of seeing his youngest son again. For days and months and years, the father had worked with one eye on the horizon, always looking for his boy. One day, working in the field, he lifted his head yet another time to scan the horizon. And there in the distance he saw a figure. The clothes were tattered; the hair, long and wild. But the father still recognized his child.

Some other father might have looked the other way in order to make his son grovel. Some other father might have met his son with a fierce frown and a stern lecture on the handling of finances. But not this father. He didn't even wait for his son to get to the house. Filled with love and pity, he ran to his son, embraced him, and kissed him.

The son pulled back, embarrassed. Wisely, his father listened as his son confessed, "Father, I have sinned against heaven and against you. I am no longer worthy to be called your son."

At that point, however, his father hushed him. "Worthy?" the father said. "What does worth have to do with being part of this family? Each member of this family belongs here, not because they have earned the right or performed to any level, but simply because they were born into it."

The older brother, however, had ideas of his own. Coming in from the fields after a long day's work, he viewed the preparations for the celebration of his brother's homecoming with disgust. Finally he pulled his father aside. "Look," he said, "I've worked hard for years and you never threw me a party. Yet my brother comes back after wasting all your money on prostitutes and drinking, and you celebrate by killing the best calf we have."

His father answered, "Son, acceptance in this family is not earned. I don't love you just because you work hard and spend your money wisely. I love you because you are my son, a part of my family. I am not rejoicing because I love your brother more than you. No—I am rejoicing because I am so glad to have a lost son back home."

An Unconditional Relationship

When John Hinckley shot President Reagan, his family did not reject him. The interviews with his parents revealed how repugnant and disgusting they found this act, for they had trained their son to know the difference between right and wrong. Yet, as painful as the ordeal was and as vile as this boy's actions were, they remained by their son's side throughout the trial. Regardless of his behavior, he was valuable to them.

Other than the family, no other relationship or membership on earth is predicated upon the fact that membership is not earned. Each family member is valuable simply because he or she is a family member—not because he or she does something well, is beautiful, or owns many possessions. The family is the only relationship on earth that has been set up to show each of us that we are valuable purely for being ourselves.

Like a teacher, the father in the parable of the Prodigal Son was responsible for training the boys. He had probably taught his wayward younger child to live a life that would bring honor to the family. The boy, however, disobeyed his father and chose his own way of life. Though the father did not approve of such behavior, he still loved him and accepted him back.

In other teacher-pupil relationships, if the pupil rebelled against the training as completely as this boy did, he would be expelled. The relationship between teacher and pupil demands that the pupil be willing to learn, and if he isn't, there can be no relationship between teacher and pupil. Not so in a healthy family relationship. Whether the child responds or not should have no bearing on the relationship. They are still family.

The father in this parable was also the employer of his sons, paying them to work his fields. Usually, when an employee loses money for the company, he is fired. After all, the employer is in the business of making money, not underwriting the escapades of one of his workers. The father therefore had every right to reject his younger son in terms of a business relationship.

The father, however, chose not to treat his son as an employee, but rather as a family member. As important as the money was, his child was far more valuable. He did not "fire" his son for irresponsible behavior. On the contrary, the father accepted his child back with open arms.

Through this parable, Jesus gave us a stunning portrait

of God the Father—a Father who has established a relationship with us that is *unconditional.* Our heavenly Father went beyond the father in the parable. Rather than wait for us to come home, he left his home in heaven to come down to earth and search for his children. He loved us so much that he sacrificed more than just a portion of the family business—he sacrificed his only Son so that each of his children could live with him forever.

Ultimately, God wants us to base our self-esteem on the truth that he is the Father and each of us is a prodigal son or daughter. The fact that the King of creation found me so valuable that he paid for my life with the life of his Son should have a profound impact on my feeling of worth and self-esteem.

PART II

How Do
I Raise
a Confident
Child?

5

SELF-ESTEEM IN THE INFANT AND TODDLER

Many years ago orphanages cared for children whose parents were dead or were, for some other reason, unable to care for them. Typically, orphanages were overcrowded. The nurses in the infant section often had so many babies to take care of that they had time only to provide the basic needs: food, warmth, and a change of diapers.

In 1945, Dr. R. A. Spitz studied orphanages to determine how well the needs of babies were being met. He found that, even in orphanages where a baby's physical needs were cared for adequately, 32 to 90 percent of the babies died before their first birthday. Obviously, some ingredient necessary to an infant's survival was missing.

Benjamin Fine validated Spitz's findings in his study of a physician working in a South American orphanage. This physician noticed that, for no apparent physical reason, many babies in the orphanage would gradually weaken and die before reaching their second birthday. Once again, the nurses in the orphanage had a heavy work load and no time to do anything but attend to the physical needs of the babies.

Both Spitz and Fine concluded that the babies died because they lacked mother-love, or a mother substitute with the time to make them feel special and valuable. When a baby is in the womb, he is attached to the mother by an umbilical cord, which serves as the channel for nourishment. When the baby is born and the umbilical cord is cut, the infant almost seems to want to reattach itself to his mother, this time for emotional nurturing. This process has been referred to as "attachment" to the parents, and if it is lacking, the very survival of the infant is threatened. An infant needs to know that he is not alone but that he intimately belongs to someone.

The mother-infant relationship is extremely important, for the newborn will instinctively try to find out who he is and how much he is loved by looking into the face of the mother, who becomes the child's mirror. As the infant looks up into the mother's face, her loving glow and warmth reflect back to the infant that, "Yes, you are very special."

"Mom the mirror" reflects back to the child that he is valuable when he wakes up from a nap, when he lies next to her in bed, when he is bathing, and many other times that are "non-performance oriented." But she also encourages the infant when he performs: rolling himself over, eating his first food, uttering his first word, and taking his first step. Thus the baby quickly learns an important lesson: he is valuable in Mom's eyes both when he performs and when he does not. He begins to realize he is special simply because he is hers.

Our self-esteem, then, begins to develop as soon as we are born—and maybe even earlier! As the mother talks to the child, helps him shake a rattle, or reads him stories, the baby grows in the knowledge of himself and his world. The activity is important, but the interaction and touching between mother and child are far more significant.

Dad is also a mirror for baby's self-esteem and contributes just as much to a child's sense of being loved and valued. Often, however, fathers are more "performance-oriented" in their response, applauding the baby only for jobs well done. Fathers may find it difficult to send back encouraging reflections simply for a baby's existence.

A baby can sense which mirror gives the best reflections. When my daughter Torrey was young she, like other babies, would wake up in the middle of the night and call for one of us. My wife, Rosemary, would go "floating" into Torrey's room, somehow in a wonderful mood. Singing little songs, she would put Torrey back to sleep. Rosemary gave the impression that even at 3:00 in the morning she was glad to have the opportunity to be with our baby.

On other occasions Torrey called for Daddy. (At least Rosemary said she did. I must confess here that I don't do well after midnight.) I would bounce off a few of the walls and, after stubbing my toes, would finally find the door to Torrey's room. Once in there, I would try to pacify the baby, shaking the crib in a less-than-gentle manner.

Torrey soon learned that Daddy's reflections were different after hours. When she didn't receive the kind of encouragement she wanted from me, she began to call only for Mommy. Only Mommy was able, or willing, to give off an unconditional positive response at that hour. So Mommy got the call. (And to this day Rosemary thinks that somehow I taught Torrey to call only Mommy after midnight!)

Conditioning Continues

Conditioning is a process whereby a response is learned when a certain behavior is consistently rewarded. For example, as a child I would tap on the top of the fish tank a few times, and when the fish came to the top I would feed them. Before long they were conditioned to respond because they liked the result—the food. Eventually they swam to the surface at just the sight of me coming toward the tank, for they were conditioned to expect food.

As a child matures, she is conditioned to respond in certain ways when she is consistently rewarded for a particular behavior. For example, a baby who is wet will cry for help. When the parent comes in to change her, she learns, or is conditioned, to cry in order to have her diaper changed. And Torrey, in the previous story, was "conditioned" to call for her mother because her mother responded positively to her late-night cries.

Toddlers use the mirror-reflection relationship to condition themselves and help them grow. When a child eats her vegetables "all gone" she looks to Mom and Dad, and their response shows her she is doing well. For example, Torrey had a unique way of getting positive feedback when she was learning to eat certain foods. A simple smile or "That's wonderful, honey" did not do it. So we created a more dynamic response. Every time she ate her vegetables, I would "honk my nose"—push my nose and honk like the "time's-up buzzer" on quiz shows. It worked beautifully. She ate all her vegetables every time. I guess she felt that she must be pretty special and the vegetables must be pretty important if I was willing to do something so incredibly ridiculous to get her to eat them. (This was a great plan until she wanted me to "honk my nose" while we were in a crowded restaurant.)

We continue to condition our toddlers to come to us for positive reflections as they come running to show us the toy they just built, the picture they just colored, or the clay figure they just molded. Hopefully, we are the mirror that is available to them almost any time of day or night, standing ready to reflect back that they are special and what they are doing is significant. Once I even received a phone call at work where one of my children proudly reported, "Daddy, I just used the potty!"

Through the early years children are being taught that they are special in the eyes of the parents. There is nothing wrong with this conditioning, for children need to be attached to their parents in order to have a healthy self-esteem. In fact, God wants parents to teach small children to look to them to find out who they are and how valuable they are. Only a parent can reflect back to the preschool-age child in a consistent, unconditional manner. The parents are God's substitutes, and we as parents are only attempting to love the children God's way, with a love that is unconditional and always available.

6

ESTABLISHING FAMILY PRIORITIES

Remember Darlene? She had been striving to be "super mom," and instead she had become a taxicab driver, dropping her children off at one activity after another. Finally she realized that other people were having more input in her children's lives than she was.

"Look at this situation," she said to her husband Jack. "Here I am carting the children around to people who will never be as dedicated to them as we are. After all, we're their *parents*."

After listening to Darlene, Jack agreed that some changes needed to be made. Together they sat down and reevaluated their purpose as parents. Jack asked, "When the Bible says, 'Train a child in the way he should go,' did God mean for the parent to do the training, or did he just want the parent to arrange for someone else to do the training?"

Darlene looked at Jack. They both knew the answer to that question.

Understanding God's will for them as parents, Jack and Darlene then began to evaluate the use of Joey's and Brenda's time. Were all the lessons and activities really necessary? Were they investing in these activities for the growth of the children, or to meet their own needs as super parents?

"What it comes down to is this," Jack said decisively,

"we have to decide whether an activity will help our children for years to come, or if it's just a time-filler."

"You're right," Darlene said. "Our being with them and loving them is more important than all these activities. We need to cut some things out."

In order to evaluate the activities, Jack and Darlene listed their children's activities in order of importance. Joey's list was first: (1) school, (2) church choir, (3) gymnastics, and (4) music lessons. Once the list was arranged in order of priority, Jack and Darlene sat eight-year-old Joey down to look at the list and rearrange the order according to his preferences.

"Put school last," Joey said, flashing them a grin.

"I don't think so," his father laughed.

Joey looked the list over again. "I think that's OK," he said hesitantly.

Jack and Darlene talked further, examining each activity to see where they could have more input. To get involved in Joey's academic training, Darlene decided to volunteer as room mother one morning a week. "Then I'll know how he's getting along with his teacher and the other students. And when he talks about other kids, I'll know who he's talking about."

Jack nodded. "I've always meant to help Joey more with his homework," he said, "but I've been to so many meetings lately—"

"Don't forget all the T.V. you watch," Darlene said. Jack grimaced. He knew she was right. He'd spent far too much time in front of the television lately.

"OK, I'll make a point of helping with the homework. It'll be tough, but I'll do it," he promised. "For Joey's sake."

"What about choir?" Darlene asked. "I think it's good for Joey—musically and spiritually. But how could we get involved? Maybe I should be a youth choir worker—"

"Don't overload *yourself* now," Jack warned. "I don't want an exhausted wife."

"You're right," she said, "I trust the choir leaders with the kids. And I like the time I have to visit with other mothers while the kids are practicing."

Gymnastics, next down on the list, involved major decisions. Two afternoons a week Joey was whisked from school to gymnastics and then home for dinner.

"The coach said the children would have to practice that often to make it in the big competitions," Jack said.

"But it's getting so it's taking over our lives," Darlene replied. "We practically have to plan our vacations around gymnastics."

After much prayer and discussion, Jack, Darlene, and Joey decided that two afternoons a week were just too much. Against the advice of the coach, they decided to cut down to one gymnastics session. The family also decided to attend as many practices and meets as possible. And Jack bought a video camera and player to videotape the gymnastics meets and other family events so that they could all enjoy watching as a family.

Trumpet lessons, last on the list, were the most difficult to let go. Both parents felt that Joey could enjoy playing his trumpet for a lifetime. They also felt, however, that Joey's week was too crowded with activities. Finally they decided to discontinue Joey's trumpet lessons until junior high.

Next Jack and Darlene evaluated Brenda's schedule and pared down her activities as they had with Joey—not because they were tired of driving her around, nor because they felt her outside activities weren't important. Rather, they felt that the family came first. Their job as parents was not just to supply a bed and meals. God lent them these two children to raise, to train, and to love, things that could not be done effectively by subcontractors.

What this one family did is not necessarily what every family should do. But this family illustrates what can be done to rectify a bad situation.

Many parents are duped into believing that their children must learn outside the home so that professionals can teach them. But there is no professional more equipped to love and train a child than her own parents. It is not a matter of whether parents *can* do something constructive with the child in the afternoon or evening. It is a question of whether parents are *willing* to make the commitment to invest in the lives of their children. After all, what could be more important than letting your child know that he or she is significant enough to be worthy of your time and companionship?

7

OPENING THE LINES OF COMMUNICATION

Several years ago, Sheridan House Ministries was approached by a group of businessmen to discuss their possible involvement with our ministry. As executive director, I listened to their proposal, but soon I realized that I needed more advice. So I asked my friend Carl, who happens to be a very wise negotiator, to sit in on the discussion.

I picked up the two business executives from the airport, and we drove to Carl's office, where we were to hold the meeting.

Our talks began at 10:00 A.M. After almost two hours, Carl said, "Gentlemen, we will need to wrap this meeting up, as I have a very important engagement for lunch this noon." But the men did not stop talking. Apparently they either had not heard or did not believe what Carl had said. But precisely at noon, Carl closed the meeting, ending with a word of prayer and a promise that we would discuss their proposal.

All four of us stood up and walked out of his office. There at the foot of the stairs was Carl's important luncheon engagement. "Gentlemen," he said, turning to us, "this is my date for lunch, my eight-year-old daughter, Laura."

You could have knocked us over with a feather. Better

yet was the look on Laura's face as she watched her daddy leave a meeting to take her to lunch.

Later on I asked Carl if this luncheon engagement was a regular activity. I'll never forget his reply. "No matter how busy I get," he said, "I make a habit of dating my children on a regular basis."

A Yes, a No, or a Grunt

Remember Jack and Darlene? When they were mere chauffeurs, they rarely talked *with* their children. Instead, they talked *at* the children. Because there was no time to sit down and discuss decisions, they rushed around telling their children to go here, go there, or hurry up. Soon Joey and Brenda learned how to be robots and respond, but they never learned to form an opinion. So when their parents began to ask their opinion about how to spend their time, at first they were at a loss. Discussions of any kind were so rare that they did not know how to do anything but respond with a yes, a no, or a grunt.

Teaching a child to communicate requires three basic ingredients: openness, listening, and time. First, the child must feel that he or she is allowed to have an opinion. If you never allow your child to present her opinions, it will quash her desire to talk to you.

Second, you need to listen—to show that you actually want to hear what your child has to say. A father came to me once and asked me to work with his child. When I asked him what was wrong, he replied, "I really don't know, except that we don't seem to communicate with each other. He never talks to me."

"You are asking me to set aside time to meet with your boy," I commented. "Do you ever do that?"

His answer was a classic: "If I set aside time with my son, what would I say to him?"

What should this father say to his son? As little as possible! All a child needs is for the parent to listen with full, undivided attention. In this way a child learns that she is valuable, that her opinion counts and is even sought after.

Third, the parent must be willing to set aside the time to listen. Once again, we are faced with that commodity we call "time." No matter how rich or poor we are, we still have only twenty-four hours in a day. And our calendars spell out loudly and clearly just what our priorities are. We must schedule time with our children if we are to open and maintain the lines of communication. Even Susanna Wesley, the mother of Charles and John Wesley and fifteen other children, set aside one hour per week to spend alone with each of her children.

How Does a Parent Date a Child?

"These are good ideas," you may be saying, "but how do I put them into practice?" Let's go back to my friend Carl. To communicate with his daughter, he "dated" her. What exactly does a parent-child date entail?

The obvious first step is to plan. A date does not happen by accident—not in our schedule-conscious world! You must plan for it, setting up a routine and scheduling it on a calendar, preferably a family calendar. We schedule our dates on a calendar on the refrigerator, so everyone in the family is reminded of this prior commitment and avoids scheduling conflicts. The calendar also serves as a tangible reminder to the children that they are so important that their parents schedule time to be with them.

Sometimes I take advantage of the calendar to give an extra boost to my children's self-esteem. Once, for example, a man called to see if I could come to a meeting that Saturday morning. I leaned over and checked the calendar. Knowing the children could hear me, I replied, "Sorry, I'd love to come, but that morning I'm having breakfast with my son Robey." When I hung up the phone, I could see the awe in my son's eyes. I could almost hear him thinking, *My dad's turning down the meeting just because he wants to be with me. Wow! I must be special.*

Once the date has been scheduled and committed to, do not break it! When I first started dating my children, I often tried to "reschedule" the date when something came up at church or work. Here I was dating my children to let them know they were special, yet unexpected phone calls continually took priority over Robey or Torrey. I bet my children thought: "We're important to Daddy just so long as nothing more important comes along."

I finally saw the mixed messages I was sending my kids. Now I rarely, if ever, "reschedule" our dates. After all, what could be more important than to have my children know I love and value them? I find now that very few things come up that are important enough to make me break our dates.

Choose the location of your date carefully. Torrey and I have gone to the movies together, but that was not a date. A date needs to be in a setting where a parent and child can talk. For some it may be a walk in the park. Others may want to fish together. The best setting I have found is a restaurant.

Ever since my children were three, we have dated by eating breakfast or lunch together. At that early age, you may feel that you are doing little more than setting a precedent—but don't give up! Dating a three-year-old has its own special charm.

I'll never forget the first time I took Robey out for lunch. He ordered a hot dog and when it arrived, he covered it with mustard. Then he carefully picked it up, aimed it at his mouth, and squeezed. Next thing I knew the hot dog had shot out of the bun and was traveling at unheard-of speeds to the edge of the table. I leaped up and caught it, mustard and all, just before it hit the floor.

Robey and I have laughed about that "disastrous" first date many times since!

Starting Conversation

Initially, getting your children to talk will be like pulling teeth, especially if they are not used to the idea. To start a conversation, you will need to ask questions that demand more than a one-word answer. I learned this lesson the hard way.

Here's what one of our early conversations may have sounded like:

DAD: Do you like our family vacations, Torrey?
TORREY: Yes.
DAD: Did you like camping last year?
TORREY: No.
DAD: Would you like to stay in a hotel instead?
TORREY: Yes.

After some practice, I learned to change my approach:

DAD: Torrey, we are trying to decide where to go on vacation this year. Do you have any suggestions?

TORREY: I don't know.

DAD: Well, we have been to several different places in the past. Which did you like best?

TORREY: Disney World! I loved all the rides and things. . . ."

At that point all I needed to do was lean back and listen to Torrey list what she liked best about our vacation to Disney World.

You may need to jump start a conversation by asking some questions, but try to stop talking as soon as possible. And be sure to leave some silence open for your child to speak. At first both of you will be uncomfortable during those silences. Your child may be used to your jumping in and supplying the answer for him. But resist the temptation.

When I give seminars I always allow time for questions at the end of each session. Often the silence dragged on so long that I would leap in, filling the silence with talk so no one would feel uncomfortable. Finally a seasoned seminar speaker came up to me after one such session. "May I give you some advice?" he said. "When you ask if there are any questions and there's a long silence, don't take the responsibility for the silence. Just wait. After a while, the audience will accept responsibility for the silence and start asking questions."

Amazingly, he was right. The very next time I spoke, I opened the floor to questions and kept quiet. The silence grew and grew, and it was almost like a game: "Who is going to break the silence first?" Finally, one person raised her hand. After that hands popped up all over.

Parents also should allow the child to decide what to do about the silence after a question. Instead of feeling compelled to rescue your child from the silence, sit quietly and wait for a response. Once your child realizes that you actually want to hear her opinion, she will open up and speak.

The Benefits of Dating

The "payoff" for dating your children may not be immediately evident. For months or even years, nothing of consequence may come up during these special dates. There may come a time, however, when your teenage daughter needs that special lunch with Mom or Dad to unload a burden. And the benefits of ongoing communication are immeasurable.

As a counselor, I am often amazed at how much people will save up from week to week to unload in their counseling session, when they feel for once that someone is really listening and truly cares. I want my children to receive the same kind of special attention I give to each of my clients. I want them to feel that if they have a problem that seems difficult to talk about, our special date is the perfect time, that it is a time when I really listen hard with my ears, eyes, and heart, that I won't interrupt or criticize. I want them to know that they are valuable and I am with them because I want to be.

When I was in high school, one of my friends had a dad who dated her once a month. They would go out to dinner to a nice restaurant, and he would always treat her like a lady.

My friend graduated from high school in the Washington, D.C., area and moved to Chicago to attend college. Over Christmas break she told me, "This past fall, Dad called to say he was planning a business trip to Chicago. And guess what? He wanted to know if I could go out to dinner on the same evening he and I used to have our special date!"

Her eyes filled up with tears. "I just couldn't believe it," she said, "and neither could any of the other kids in the dorm. My roommates kept saying, 'You must really be important to your parents.'

"When he came to the dorm to pick me up, I was so excited. I guess for the first time in my life I realized how special my dad thought I was. We had the greatest talk we had ever had that night at dinner."

My friend and her father enjoyed good communication on their dates. They enjoyed quality time together. But most of all, they enjoyed the greatest benefit of dating: a loving father-daughter relationship.

8

CREATING A STRONG
FAMILY TEAM

"What have you done lately to make your family feel like they are different from all the other families on the block?" I asked at the end of a seminar titled "Making Your Family Special."

"Last weekend we had what we called a 'Little House on the Prairie' weekend," one man answered. "We all stayed home for the weekend, and starting on Friday night, we converted our home into a 'Little House on the Prairie.' We shut off the electricity, and my wife cooked dinner on the grill. We lit candles to eat by and to wash the dishes. At first the kids seemed to enjoy it, but later on in the evening they disappeared into their rooms, and I caught them using a battery-operated flashlight and a battery-operated transistor radio. So I went through the house and confiscated all the batteries.

"The children dragged into the kitchen, complaining and begging us to turn on the electricity. 'All right, let's talk about it,' I said. We lit a few more candles, and the whole family sat down to discuss the weekend. At first I thought that we were headed for a disaster, but slowly I realized that we were doing exactly what had always seemed so appealing on the television show: we were finally sitting around the kitchen table talking. To my amazement, the whole family stayed around the table, talking, sharing, and laughing for the next two and a half hours.

"That night was only the beginning of a fantastic weekend. Not only did we all commit ourselves to do it again every few months, but my children—and I guess even I—couldn't wait to tell friends what a special thing our family had done."

The Most Innovative Family Around

Earlier I made the point that our self-esteem is affected by the groups to which we belong. Corporations know this and work very hard at making their employees feel they are a part of the most innovative and successful company around. This kind of interoffice propaganda makes people feel that they belong to a winner and they work all the harder to do their part to keep their company ahead.

Athletic coaches operate much the same way. If the team feels it is the best, then it certainly stands a better chance of becoming the best. It is one of the coach's jobs to instill in the athletes that kind of pride and confidence.

A college football coach once said that he did not choose high-school football candidates on their ability alone. "If they have the ability but their self-esteem is low from being on losing teams, I don't want them," he stated.

If feeling like a winner is so important for business and athletics, how much more important is it for the family! Children need to feel that they belong to a family that is special and functioning as a team.

Unfortunately, some families act more like guests in a boarding house than families. With little sense of family cohesion or distinctiveness, children in these families will begin to feel that they aren't very special. And because they lack the sense of belonging to something special, they begin to search for groups outside the home to join, not caring whether these outside groups are good or bad. Their search for self-esteem—wanting to belong *somewhere*—often touches off much pain and heartache for the whole family.

The Test for a Strong Family Team

How do we know if our family is functioning like a positive team? First ask yourself: Is your family special?

1. During holidays could one of your children walk into any house in the neighborhood and find the celebration handled exactly the same way, with only the faces changed? Is Thanksgiving at your house like Thanksgiving at everyone else's house—turkey and then back to the television—or do you have special family traditions?
2. Do your children have to go to someone else's house to laugh or have a good time? Has it been a long time since your family has had a good laugh together?
3. Does the family ever spend an evening together playing games, reading, or doing some activity other than watching TV?
4. Do the children get behind each other's activities and accomplishments, or do they constantly ridicule and belittle one another?
5. Does the family ever do anything as a team, or is it always "every man for himself" on weekends?

In many homes today people don't make time for special activities, and the self-esteem of the children suffers as a result.

Great Projects

Our eighteen-year-old baby-sitter, Barbie, had always been a special person. A very attractive girl, she seemed the type that would be swamped with dates. Yet she usually preferred to do things with her family on Friday and Saturday nights. She had an older and younger brother, but sibling rivalry never seemed like a problem in her family. Finally, out of curiosity, I asked her, "Do you ever fight with your brothers?"

Barbie laughed. "Oh, sure, we have arguments every once in a while."

I pressed the issue. "What makes your family so special?"

Barbie smiled. "My dad and mom are always dreaming up great projects for the whole family to do. One year Dad brought home a beat-up old boat that we all spent our spare time repairing. Then we took it down to the Florida Keys. Another summer the whole family took scuba lessons and spent our vacation diving and catching lobsters.

"One of the best projects was preparing for our trip to the Smithsonian Institute," she said. "Each of us sent away for information on a specific section of the Smithsonian. I got brochures on the Hall of Presidents and one of my brothers got information on the Aerospace Museum. As we got closer to vacation time we began to give reports on what we were reading. Most fun of all, however, was to get there and actually see what we had been reading about. Then each of us became the tour guide for our family when we got to our particular section of the Smithsonian.

"I've just always found it fun to be with my family because we work as a team. I like my friends at school and church, and I have fun with them, but it's different with my family. We work together, and I feel like my mom and dad and two brothers think I'm important. I'm not competing against my brothers, so it helps us get along. I'm sure some of my friends get away from their families on Friday and Saturday nights just to find friendship. But my family members are my best friends."

Barbie taught me a lot about healthy families in that one small conversation. Because her family worked as a team, there was little fighting between siblings. Instead of five individuals competing against each other, her family was going in one direction, headed for a common goal. Barbie, as a result, had no need to look outside her family for a place to belong. Her search for self-esteem remained in the hands of those who loved her the most—her family.

Family Traditions

My wife's family has always been very close, and one of the reasons is that they have grown up rich in traditions. Christmas, especially, was a time for special family celebrations.

Just before my first Christmas with her family, Rosemary tried to prepare me for the traditions I would now take part in. "First," she said, "we go to our church's candlelight Christmas Eve service. After the service, we put on special flannel pajamas and open one present. Then we read the Christmas passage in Luke, read *'Twas the Night before Christmas*, hang our stockings on the mantle, and go to bed."

She talked about these traditions as if they were sacred! Shaking my head, I said, "But Rosemary, your three brothers are all adults now. Surely they don't still get into their flannel pajamas after church!"

She just smiled and said, "Well, let's see what happens."

Christmas Eve came and, sure enough, at 7:30, we all climbed into the car and headed for the candlelight service. I wasn't too worried about the rest of the traditions coming to fruition, however, because her brothers were all married, over six feet tall, and responsible adults. Besides, I didn't even own flannel pajamas.

When we returned from church everyone vanished into their rooms. We were all spending the night at her parents' house, so I just walked into the living room and sat down by the Christmas tree with my suit coat and tie on, like any civilized individual. Moments later, three generations of Johnsons descended upon the living room, all wearing flannel pajamas.

They sat down, almost ignoring my presence. Then it came time for the opening of one Christmas Eve present. There was the traditional arguing of "Why don't we open more than one this year?" and just as traditionally, that request was denied. It was almost as if they were following a script.

They handed me the first present to be unwrapped. The room got quiet as I removed the paper and lifted the lid of the box. Then the whole family burst into laughter. There, in the box, was a pair of flannel pajamas! As if that weren't enough, they refused to open another present until I had donned my new Johnson family Christmas uniform.

Traditions are important to families because they make one family different from another. They are the glue that keeps a family together. Rosemary's brothers are married and live all over the country. They did not return home for Christmas simply to give and take presents. Christmas at their house was special, so they wanted to be there.

Children will not ask for traditions, nor will they say thank you when they are incorporated into the family's schedule. My mother-in-law learned that one Christmas.

Every Christmas Mrs. Johnson would get tickets for the whole family to go to Handel's *Messiah*. And every year the boys would complain, "Not again! Do we have to go again this year?" They complained continuously. They even complained in the car on the way to the concert. It got so bad that one year Mrs. Johnson did not bother to get the tickets. As the time got close to Christmas Day, however, the boys realized they had not yet gone to hear *The Messiah*.

Finally one of them asked, "Mom, when are we going to *The Messiah?*"

Mrs. Johnson replied, "I thought I wouldn't bother you with it this year, so I didn't get the tickets."

You would have thought that Christmas itself had been cancelled! Instantly they began to cry, "We have to go to *The Messiah!* We *always* do. We never mean what we say about not wanting to go."

At this point, Mrs. Johnson realized that the complaining of the past was actually a tradition *in itself* to tease her. The boys were truly upset that the tradition of going to this event had been broken. She had thought she would relieve her boys of a burden. Not so! They were secure in the routine of the tradition. It made their family feel special.

Not only can traditions be developed for holidays, but also for seasons of the year. Each season in my home, the children set aside an afternoon with Rosemary to collect the knickknacks and crafts of the previous season and put out the new ones. At the end of fall, Robey, Torrey, and Rosemary pack away the ceramic pumpkins, Indian corn, cornucopia centerpiece, and exchange them all for the winter decorations. This whole process takes an entire afternoon, and when I arrive home the children are beside themselves waiting to take me on a tour.

Traditions can also be incorporated into the weekly routine. Every Sunday morning I walk to church with the children, and Rosemary drives to church later on. The children never say to me, "Boy, it was sure great walking to church again today, Dad. I'm glad we always do that." The only way I know that they cherish this routine is that they get visibly depressed when rain cancels our Sunday morning walk.

Several years ago, a sixteen-year-old girl came to live with us for about six months, and she had to take part in our family traditions, like game night and our daily family meeting.

At her first game night Bonnie sat like a bump on a log. A game of Flinch was far beneath her dignity, and she refused to get overly involved. So I decided to just lean over and take a good look at her cards.

"Hey, what do you think you're doing?" she demanded, pulling back her cards.

"Nothing," I replied innocently.

A little later I peeked again. "Stop that!" she cried.

"If you don't mind," I said, "it would help my game if I could see your cards."

"No way!" she retorted.

I shrugged. "I really didn't think you cared."

But after that, she did. We all laughed when I tried to sneak a glance, and sometimes Bonnie even tried to tempt me into looking at her cards.

But our family meetings each morning had the biggest impact on Bonnie. Every morning our family gathers for family devotions, then talks together before we all go off to face the day. Initially Bonnie did not know what to make of this "daily team huddle." Slowly, however, Bonnie became a part of our home, dropping her sullen face and adopting the attitude of her new "team." As she grew more positive, so did we!

Bonnie is married now and has a family of her own. She and Rosemary are very close, and though it has been many years since she lived with us, she still comments every now and then on our tradition of morning meetings. They meant a lot to her because they made her feel like a real member of our family.

Finally, traditions can be made when families work as a team to help others. One week before the Christmas season, Rosemary suggested to the family that we bake cookies, put them in special decorative tins, and give them away to our neighbors. We were 100 percent behind her, until she said, "give them away."

That Saturday the whole family spent the day rolling out the dough, cutting special Christmas designs, and then popping them into the oven. We sang Christmas carols and thoroughly enjoyed ourselves, and when nobody else was watching each of us managed to eat a fair amount of cookie dough! But then came the part that no one but Rosemary was overly excited about. We had put the finished cookies into the decorated tins, and it was time to deliver them to our neighbors.

The plan was to walk up to each house, knock on the door, and when the door opened, sing the chorus from "We Wish You a Merry Christmas." Then we would hand our neighbor the cookies and say, "Merry Christmas."

As we went out the door to our first neighbor, the children were visibly depressed about giving away all their cookies. And I was not overly excited about singing on my neighbors' front yards.

To top it off, our nearest neighbor was an elderly single Jewish woman who had been a prisoner in a World War II German concentration camp. We walked up to her door,

Torrey staring wistfully at the tin of cookies in her hand. Just as I knocked on the door, I saw a menorah lit in the window. She was celebrating Hanukkah, an important Jewish holiday. Wow! My heart was in my throat when the door opened.

Rosemary burst into the chorus of "We Wish You a Merry Christmas." The children whispered the tune while they looked at their cookies, and I mumbled in the background, hoping that no one was watching. When the song—virtually a solo by Rosemary—was finished, Torrey reluctantly handed the cookies to our neighbor.

Her lips trembled. Her eyes filled with tears. Over and over, she thanked us for remembering her with the cookies.

Needless to say, the children could not wait to distribute the rest of the cookies. That night as we walked home we knew that something special had taken place. As a team working together, we had ministered to our neighbors. We had learned that it is more blessed to give than to receive. The children gave their prized cookies, and I gave my pride! That year was the start of an ongoing tradition, and now even *I* sing out when we deliver the cookies.

PART III

How Do I Teach My Child Responsibility?

9

THE NEED FOR RESPONSIBILITY

"Excuse me, could we talk to you for a second?"

I looked up from my desk to see Mr. and Mrs. Barnhart. Their son, Jamie, had lived at Sheridan House for only a month, and he had recently been able to spend a weekend home with his parents.

"Sure, come in," I replied. "Is there a problem with Jamie?"

"No, that's just it," said Mr. Barnhart. "We'd like to discuss Jamie's sudden, or should I say, tremendous improvement in attitude. There's not a problem with Jamie, but we were wondering if there is a problem with us."

As the Barnharts sat down in my office, I asked them what kind of attitude change they had noticed in Jamie. "We don't quite know what to make of it," Mrs. Barnhart replied. "Jamie has been a very sullen child for a couple of years now. We have tried everything we could think of to make life easier for him."

"That's right," Mr. Barnhart chimed in. "When I was a boy I was up at dawn helping out around the farm. It seemed like I worked all the time. When Jamie was born, I swore I would never make my son work as much as I had. I wanted Jamie to have a better life—to have the chance to be a child. So we take care of the chores, and he gets to spend his time doing the things I never got to do."

"Well, Jamie just got worse and worse." Mrs. Barnhart sighed. "It got so that he wouldn't touch his room or even bring a dirty glass back into the kitchen. He seemed to get more and more depressed."

"That's just it," Mr. Barnhart interrupted. "What did he have to be depressed about? We weren't making any demands on him. Jamie had it made."

"Then he became rebellious," Mrs. Barnhart said. "That was even worse than his being depressed."

After listening to their story I asked, "But what has happened that has you so puzzled?"

They told me that Jamie had taken them on a tour of Sheridan House before he left to go home with them for the weekend. First stop was the bedroom. The astonished parents saw an immaculate carpet, beds on which you could bounce a quarter, and neatly folded clothes in the closet and drawers.

Then he took them to the kitchen. At first they saw nothing out of the ordinary except that it was extremely clean and organized. "This is a very nice kitchen, Jamie," said Mrs. Barnhart, trying to act as enthusiastic as her son.

"Does it look clean, Mom?" asked Jamie.

"Yes, it looks clean, Jamie. It looks spotless," replied Mrs. Barnhart.

"Son," asked Mr. Barnhart, "did you clean this kitchen?"

The Barnharts hadn't seen such excitement in their son in years. "Yeah, Dad," he replied, "this is my responsibility every morning and every evening. And I do it so that you could eat off of the floor!"

In my office, the Barnharts laughed at the memory. "At home he complained a little about the work here, but I could still see a new Jamie," said Mrs. Barnhart. "He seemed to feel good about himself. He didn't even argue when we brought him back here. He seemed to feel like he was needed here."

Mr. Barnhart nodded. "All Jamie's life I have tried to make it easy for him. I didn't want him to have to work like I did, or have all the responsibility I had. Yet that kind of life made him feel miserable and worthless. Then he came to Sheridan House, where he has to get up at 5:30 in the morning to clean a kitchen, and he feels and looks like a new boy! For some reason Jamie did not feel he was special at home. Here at Sheridan House you've made him feel needed. In my love for my child, I've been his worst enemy."

"Mr. Barnhart," I responded, "you have obviously done a good job of showing Jamie you love him or he would not have been so excited to show you what he has done. Your mistake came in denying him the opportunity to help out in your family. Children will never ask for chores. In fact, they will usually complain about having to do them. However, regular chores are a very necessary part of a child's self-esteem development. Jamie, like each of us, needs to be able to get involved and contribute to the family."

The Need to Be Needed

Mr. and Mrs. Barnhart had honorable intentions, but they did not understand a basic need that all humans have—the need to feel needed and important. A child wants to contribute to the family in a meaningful way. In generations past this was not a common problem. Children were needed on the family farm or in the family business. Older siblings took care of younger siblings. And with the lack of modern appliances, children needed to help more with chores around the house.

Today, however, things are very different. Children are made to feel as though they are in the way when it comes to chores and responsibilities around the house. A family on my block has three sons: a twelve-year-old, a sixteen-year-old, and an eighteen-year-old. Each boy is capable of taking care of the lawn, and yet the parents have a lawn service do it. Why? Probably because it became such a hassle trying to get the boys to do it that the parents just gave up. Besides, the lawn service does the job better.

I could not count how many times I have heard a parent say, "It's just easier for me to do the dishes. My child always makes such a mess of it anyway." Or "I wash the car myself because I can do it quicker and my children never did it right anyway."

Once again, the performance becomes more important than the child. Of course an adult can do family chores better than a child. It is not the finished *product* that is of primary importance, however. It is the *process* of doing chores that is important, helping the child mature and develop into a responsible and capable adult.

The child's self-esteem is more important than a perfect lawn, an immaculate car, or spotless dishes. In the process of teaching your child to do the chore, you will help him feel he is a significant part of the family.

But What If the Child Doesn't Want To?

When she was eight my daughter came to me and said, "Daddy, can I talk to you for a minute? I now realize that chores help me develop into a responsible individual. With that in mind, I would like you to give me more chores to do."

Anyone who believes that story is wasting time reading this book! No child on earth wants to do chores—at least not after the novelty wears off. But that doesn't mean that chores are not good for children.

When Torrey was little all she wanted to eat was cookies and ice cream. But I did not give in to her and say, "OK, Torrey, since you don't like to eat vegetables and fruit, you don't have to anymore." Because I love her and know what she needs, I made a decision that was contrary to her wishes.

A few weeks before Torrey started kindergarten, she had to go to the doctor for her shots. She did not want to go to the doctor at all, and I didn't relish taking her. But I knew that for her to grow up in a healthy body, she needed the shots.

The same is true for a child and chores. Children want chores about as much as they want to eat spinach or get shots, yet they need chores for their own well-being. They need chores around the home to help them develop self-esteem and responsibility.

10

HOW TO TEACH RESPONSIBILITY

When a boy first arrives at Sheridan House, one of the first things we do is assign him a chore. We explain the chore and ask if he has any questions about it. Then we tell him that he must complete the chore by a certain time without our reminding him. In fact, we don't mention the chore again until after it is supposed to have been done. "It is your *responsibility* to remember to do the chore," we tell the boy. "If you forget, you will be denied privileges."

When Brian came to Sheridan House, I assigned him the chore of washing the van sometime between Monday and Friday afternoon at 3:30. "You may choose a time after school to do it, and when you finish, you have to ask Pop, your housefather, to check the job. And Brian, let me say this just one more time. You do understand that no one will be reminding you about this job. It is your responsibility to remember to do it and it is your responsibility to complete the chore properly, which means having it checked when you are finished. If you fail to do this, you are choosing to give up some privileges."

Brian nodded his head as have hundreds of boys before him. His eyes said, "Who me, forget? Are you kidding?"

Well, that was on Monday, and sure enough, Friday rolled around with the van still unwashed. All week Brian had seen other boys, who had been around Sheridan House longer, completing their chores. Brian, however, put off doing it the first day, and forgot about it the second day. By the time Friday came, the chore had not been completed. When I confronted Brian about his failure to be responsible for his chore, he gave the same answer that we have all used a hundred times: "I forgot."

"Brian," Pop said, "by choosing not to do your chore, you have chosen not to get an allowance this week and not to receive the other privileges that go along with it. I wish you had chosen differently, but you didn't. Next week your chore will be to cut the lawn out front of the house, and since you have chosen not to complete this week's chore of washing the van, you must do the van as well as the lawn."

Try as he might, Brian could not change this situation. He could not talk Pop out of these consequences because Pop did not choose them—Brian did.

To develop self-discipline and responsibility, Brian first had to remember the job. Then he had to choose when to do it. And finally, he needed to complete the chore. We did not follow along behind him, reminding him and nagging him to do his jobs, because that would accomplish nothing but to get a job done, and we care more about teaching the *process* of responsibility to a child than in having a completed *product*.

When the Responsibility Is Accepted

In the coming weeks, Brian chose on his own to complete the chore before Friday. Then we began the process of *encouragement*, making him aware that he was doing the right thing.

When I first came to Sheridan House, I carried around a little yellow pad to scribble encouraging notes to boys who were acting responsibly. If Brian decided to wash the van on Wednesday, the next day he would find one of my yellow notes on his bed saying, "You did a great job on the van, Brian. Thank you for accepting the responsibility to get it done two days early. Mr. Barnes."

When I wrote these notes to the boys, we could actually see their behavior change. Yet not once did a boy come up to me and say, "Mr. Barnes, your yellow note was a great encouragement to me. It had a profound effect on my desire to become a responsible individual. Thank you for taking the time out of your busy day to write it."

No, I never got any feedback from my yellow notes of encouragement. When I ran out of yellow notepads, I quit writing notes, assuming that the boys did not care about them anyway.

Several weeks later, I was sitting in a bedroom with a boy helping him pack his clothes. He had completed the program at Sheridan House, and it was time to go home. As he opened a drawer, I saw a glimmer of yellow way back in the corner of his drawer. It was a stack of the yellow notes of encouragement he had received. He had saved them like little trophies. How foolish I had been to think that encouragement meant nothing to children!

Teaching your child responsibility through family chores gives you a great opportunity to say special things like "Thank you" or "You did a nice job" or "My car has never looked so good." Chores help people see they are part of a team, and they create a ready-made opportunity to encourage the team members.

How Young Should Chores Begin?

Fred and Jill were tired of nagging their three-year-old daughter, Jennifer, about picking up her toys. Several times a day, they had to say, "Jennifer, come here and pick up this toy! How many times do I have to tell you to put your toys away when you are through playing with them?" They knew that nagging only made *them* responsible for putting away the toys, that it wasn't teaching Jennifer responsibility, and that it hurt Jennifer's self-esteem. So even though Jennifer was only three, her parents decided to teach her responsibility by giving her a chore.

"Jennifer," said Jill, "Your daddy and I are not here to walk behind you all day and pick up your toys when you're through playing with them. We would like for you to put away each toy when you are done with it. Wouldn't you like to help Mommy and Daddy by taking care of your own toys?"

Fred went into the garage and got a big box. He showed the box to Jennifer. "This box will help you do a good job of putting your toys away, " Jennifer's dad said. "Instead of yelling at you about your toys, we are going to play a game to help you learn how to take care of them. Here's how the game works. We will put this box up on the shelf in the garage. Whenever we find one of your toys lying around we will pick it up for you and put it in the box. Your toy will stay in the box until Saturday. Do you understand, Honey? Wouldn't it be wonderful if you put all your toys away and there were no toys left out to put in the box?"

This game did not work overnight, and many tears were shed in the process. Eventually, however, Jennifer learned to put away her toys because her parents were committed to the process and handled it in a very consistent manner. They also looked for every opportunity to encourage her with statements like "Honey, I am very proud of the way you just put that toy away. Thank you for being such a helper." To an adult that form of encouragement may seem ridiculous. To a child, however, those words are priceless.

With her parent's encouragement, Jennifer quickly learned personal responsibility. In fact, she almost learned *too* well. Once she found her father's shoes lying about, and she carried them to her mother. "Daddy's shoes were by the front door," she announced. "We need a box to help Daddy put his shoes away."

Jennifer is an excellent example of the fact that preschoolers are able to learn the concept of responsibility. Unfortunately, many parents wait until their child is an adolescent before they attempt to teach this concept. By then, it is long overdue.

How to Teach Responsibility

Teaching a child responsibility involves four *E*s: Example, Exposure, Experience, and Encouragement.

The first E is Example. The old adage, "Do what I say, not what I do," will definitely not work when training children. Those little ones are watching to see how we live, not listening to how we say they should live. The first step toward teaching a child anything is to be an example of what you want to teach.

The second E is Exposure. If I want a child to learn how to do something, I must do it with her for a period of time, showing her the task so she knows exactly how to do it.

The third E is Experience. Once the parent is confident that the child has mastered a skill, the parent must then withdraw from the scene so the child can practice the skill without parental interference. The child needs the opportunity to do the task, to suffer failures, and to experience the joy of completing a task successfully without help.

The fourth E is Encouragement. Parents must not forget to encourage their children every step of the way. Encouragement is not only for the successes, but also for the attempts. It cannot be overemphasized how important this fourth aspect of the training process is. Encouragement is the spark that keeps a child willing to try.

When Torrey was getting ready to go to kindergarten, Rosemary and I decided to give her a daily chore. After we talked with her, we assigned her the chore of making her bed. We took Torrey into her bedroom and showed her how to do this task, and for several mornings we helped her make her bed (exposure). Obviously she was not able to make a wrinkle-free bed right away. However, we were more interested in her learning the concept of responsibility.

After a while, Rosemary and I withdrew and let Torrey make the bed on her own (experience). At first she would call us in to see how she had done, excited and proud at doing it herself. We praised her for helping the family (encouragement), and she left for school feeling good about herself.

After several weeks, however, Torrey slacked off. She didn't seem to think the chore was very important anymore. Then we realized that we had forgotten one of the *E*s of training: Example. Rosemary and I expected Torrey to make her bed before breakfast, yet we often waited to make ours. There may have been some good reasons why our bed wasn't made until later, but to Torrey, the fact that we did not set a good example discouraged her from making her bed.

As parents, we will not be able to exemplify all the behavior we want from our growing children, but we should certainly try to do everything we can to be a good example. To teach responsibility, parents themselves have to accept responsibility within the family.

11

HOW TO DISCIPLINE

"We don't want to stifle Billy with too many rules. That's why we don't discipline him. We want him to grow up to be a confident young man, able to make decisions on his own. If we make all his decisions for him and structure his life, won't that just make him overly dependent on us?"

Randy and Sarah Talbot had come to see me about their eight-year-old son, Billy. Life with him had grown unbearable. "Our house is in a turmoil. We're at each other's throats constantly," Randy said.

"Billy won't do anything without an argument," Sarah broke in. "He won't even get up in the morning for school without a fight. We have gotten to the point where we start every day screaming at each other."

Then Randy said, "We must be doing something wrong. This constant bickering can't be good for Billy, and it's horrible for our family. I hate to send him off to school every day from this kind of tense atmosphere. What can we do?"

"Mrs. Talbot," I said, "who is responsible for Billy getting up each morning?"

"Billy is. I go into his room and call him and he is supposed to get up."

"After you go in," I probed, "what happens next? Does Billy get up?"

"Not until I've gone in several times, and I'm so exasperated that we scream at each other."

"You say that it is Billy's responsibility to get up in the morning," I said. "Yet you really don't allow him to make that decision. Actually you are accepting complete responsibility for his getting out of bed. You have become his personal 'snooze alarm,' and when you have gone back into his room enough times and become so loud he can't bear it any longer, then he knows he must get up. Both you and Billy lose all integrity in this situation. My suggestion is that you allow Billy the opportunity of being responsible for getting out of bed each morning. Don't rob him of that responsibility."

Placing Responsibility Where It Belongs

"Today when you go home, have a family meeting," I advised. "Announce to Billy that you are going to use a new system for helping him get out of bed in the morning. If I were you, I would even start by apologizing for the way mornings have been handled in the past, saying that you are sorry that you have often yelled at Billy. Tell him that you love him and want the mornings to be special, so you are going to set up a new way of operating the home so that he will be happier.

"Tell him this: 'Billy, we will no longer be coming into your room five or six times to wake you up. That's not fair to any of us. One of us will come in one time, sit on the side of your bed, and wake you up. At that point you will have fifteen minutes to get up and get to the breakfast table. If you do not get up and come to breakfast, we will not be coming back into your room until after breakfast is over. At that point I will stand in your room with you to help you get up and get dressed before going off to school.

Do you understand that I will not be coming back into your bedroom over and over? If you are unable to get up when I call you the first time, we will assume that it is because you are not getting enough sleep. The days that you don't get up you will need to go to bed at 7:30 that night instead of your usual bedtime of 8:30. Do you understand this new plan, Billy? Do you understand that the time you go to bed each night will be up to you? If you don't get up, *you will be choosing* to go to bed early."

Billy's parents loved the idea, but I could see that more explanation was necessary, so I continued. "Mrs. Talbot, this is only the beginning of the plan. Most likely Billy will leave the meeting with the best intentions of accepting the responsibility for his behavior. Then morning will roll around. You will go into his room, sit on his bed, wake him up, and walk out praying that he will get up. Five minutes later, you will peek into his room only to find that your fears have been realized—he is still in bed.

"You must resist going back into the room," I warned. "Although you may think the plan hasn't worked, the plan hasn't even begun yet. Your heart will tell you, 'Maybe he didn't hear me,' and you know that's ridiculous. When your motherly instincts and old habits try to force you to walk back into his room, stop yourself. Do not accept the responsibility for Billy's behavior. Billy needs to start making these decisions for his own self-respect.

"Now, breakfast will roll around, and Billy probably won't be up yet. As a mother, you will be anxious, because you are sending your little boy off to school without breakfast. Breakfast is important, yes, but not as important as teaching a child to be responsible. So have your breakfast, then go into Billy's bedroom, wake him up, and stay there until he is ready for school. But watch your attitude. A bad attitude is not a part of the new program, and anger and arguing should not be one of the consequences for Billy's disobedience.

"After dinner that night you may notice a marked change in Billy's behavior. He may become very helpful or solicitous. One mother using this plan told me that her son even came up to her after dinner and said, 'Mom, do you want to play a game of Monopoly tonight?' when for years she had been trying to get him to do things with the family. Well, Billy may suddenly act like your best friend, but how he behaves toward you at this point doesn't matter. As parents who love him, you want to save him the future agony of wondering whether he is truly to be held responsible for his behavior.

"Your response to him must be 'Billy, I wish we could do other things tonight, but we can't because *you* have chosen to go to bed early. In fact, it is after 7:00 now, so it's time to take your bath and get ready for bed.'

"If Billy is like most other children, he will look crushed and betrayed, and pull out all the stops to get you to change your mind. He will probably beg for one more chance, say he forgot, or tell you, 'Mom, if you just let me go this time and I ever forget to wake up again, you can give my dog away!'

"At this point the real test of who is doing the punishing takes place. Is it a parent's choice to decide whether or not to uphold consequences? If so, then the parent is showing her son that he really has no responsibility for his behavior. She can decide at a whim or according to her mood to change the rules as she chooses. This kind of parent confuses the child and encourages him to argue. What has he got to lose? After all, the consequences have little to do with his behavior. What really counts is who wins the argument.

"This kind of inconsistent setup damages the self-esteem of both child and parent. In fact, it is a horrible form of emotional child abuse, because the child sees no consistent reason other than argument deciding his fate. What a horrible way to live!

"There can be no ifs, ands, or buts," I continued. "At this point Billy—not you—has chosen to be put to bed early. To go against the rules now will ruin the plan.

"Billy will drag off to bed whining, 'It's not fair' or 'How can I sleep when it's still light outside?' As he tries to burden you with the responsibility for his plight, gently put it right back on his shoulders. Say, 'Son, we did not choose for you to go to bed at this hour—*you* did. We love you enough that we will no longer yell at you in the morning. Instead, every time you choose not to get up when you are called, and I mean *every* time, you will be choosing to go to bed early. Please don't force us to have to put you to bed early tomorrow night.'

"Mr. and Mrs. Talbot, you will be able to encourage Billy because you are no longer a part of the consequence. He is not fighting you. He is fighting a plan and his responsibility for his behavior. This frees you up to encourage him."

Randy and Sarah Talbot went home excited to begin the new plan. The plan did not work right away, however. In fact, it took a couple of weeks for Billy to realize that his parents were serious about the transfer of responsibility. Then one morning it happened. Billy actually got up before breakfast and came to the table. He was half dressed, and his hair was matted to his head, but he had made an effort to come. Mrs. Talbot jumped up, gave him a hug, and thanked him for trying.

Sound corny? Sure it is, but it got the point across. That night after dinner Mr. Talbot told Billy to hop in the tub so he could be in bed by 7:30, and Billy protested, "But, Dad,

I got up on time!" That was the first time his parents knew that Billy had accepted his new responsibility.

"Oh, that's right!" Mr. Talbot laughed. "Well, I think that we should celebrate! Let's make some popcorn and do something special. It sure is great to be able to have you up for the extra hour."

Did all this work? Certainly. Billy now saw the advantages of learning to be responsible. He saw that his parents loved him enough to set boundaries for his behavior. When he stepped over those boundaries he would be choosing to accept the consequences.

Under this system of placing the responsibility where it belongs, Billy can grow up in a secure environment where he knows the rules and what the consequences will be if *he* chooses to break them. Mom and Dad are more secure because they too know the rules and are not as frustrated when the child tests those boundaries. A family that operates like this will have a strong self-esteem. And the child will know, "Mommy's not doing this to me because she hates me, but because she loves me and always punishes me when I do this."

The mandate for orderly, loving structure is found in Ephesians 6:4: "And now a word to you parents. Don't keep on scolding and nagging your children, making them angry and resentful. Rather, bring them up with the loving discipline the Lord himself approves, with suggestions and godly advice" (LB). God instructs parents not to confuse or exasperate children with vague, inconsistent rules. To raise a confident child, parents must provide structure and discipline in the child's life. Children need a home where there are rules they can understand and where they are held responsible for their behavior. When the child does not abide by the rules, she must be consistently, but lovingly, admonished.

12

WHERE DOES SPANKING FIT IN?

In college and graduate school, I was hesitant to consider spanking as a viable form of punishment. I agreed with all the standard responses to spanking. "Spanking is so barbaric," I'd heard people say. "Doesn't spanking just teach a child how to hit?" others would ask. "I believe spanking is abusive to the child!" some would declare.

True, spanking can be done in a barbaric way, and many children have been physically abused by parents who beat them, rather than spanked them, with the wrong motives and in the wrong manner. However, children will learn how to hit whether they have been spanked or not!

Many other objections to spanking have been raised over the past three decades. And those objections are raised with good motives; children are very precious to us, and no one wants to see even one child abused. And spanking *can* be abusive. Spanking that is not done for the purpose of instruction is abusive. Spanking that is not established as a consistent consequence ahead of time is abusive. Spanking done in rage or anger is abusive.

Spanking that is done in a loving and immediate manner, however, is the most effective discipline for the child. Instead of verbally berating the child or delaying the punishment—thus forcing the child to feel guilty and "bad" for a longer period of time—immediate spanking allows the child to feel immediately forgiven. Immediate spanking, a consequence that follows bad behavior, shows the child that it is the behavior that is bad, not the child.

The Best Form of Punishment

I wish I could say that I learned about spanking from years of study. I did not, however. It took three real-life instances to teach me that spanking is the most merciful form of punishment for a child.

My first experience came in 1974, when I was hired as the new director of Sheridan House for Boys. At that time we had only one home for boys on our property. Two weeks after I arrived, our houseparents resigned. Until we were able to locate and train new houseparents, I would have to move in and become the houseparent.

There was no formal education in the world that could have prepared me for that forty-five-day experience. I kissed my wife, Rosemary, good-bye and moved into that boys' home, feeling as if I were being sent to stand alongside General Custer. And, sure enough, that very first night the battle began.

At 9:00 the twelve boys were watching television. Walking into the living room, I announced, "It's time for bed, boys. Turn off the television and let's call it a night."

They all started in that direction, so I turned around feeling successful and walked back into my office. I was about to sit down when I heard a funny noise. Was that a laugh track I heard?

The boys must have gone to bed without turning off the television, I said to myself as I got up to turn it off. But there, smack dab in the middle of the living room, were all the boys—still sitting there watching television.

This time when I walked into the room the atmosphere was tense. Obviously they had had a meeting and decided to ignore me. In my graduate school naivete, I thought that we would be able to circle up, hold group therapy, and deal with the rebellion. At least, that was what many of my textbooks had told me.

But one look around the room told me that group therapy wouldn't work here. By their actions they were asking a simple question: "Who's in charge here?" I could see that the boys were extremely uncomfortable and insecure about the situation—all except Alfred. As I had guessed earlier, he was the ringleader.

When I had failed to get anyone's attention over the sound of the television, I walked over and turned the set off. The boys just looked at me. I announced, "Everyone needs to be in bed, under the covers, in five minutes. I will spank whoever is not."

I could not believe that the word *spank* had actually come out of my mouth! I wanted to turn around and see if maybe someone behind me had said it! Better yet, if someone behind me would *do* it if need be!

The word *spank* broke the spell in that room. The boys were up and off to bed, and you could see the relief on their faces. Finally, a mature adult had ended the conflict.

I followed them into their rooms. When I came back, it was to see one lone boy still sitting in front of the television. Alfred.

My heart sank.

I knew that Alfred needed more concrete evidence than simply my word. He was interested in finding out, firsthand, if I was committed enough to follow through on my statement. I walked up to the television, turned it off, and escorted Alfred into my office. He did anything he could think of to avoid being spanked. Finally, however, he consented to the spanking, and I paddled him. We then sat down on the couch together and I told him that I had forgiven him for his rebellion.

"Alfred," I said, "I am confident your rebellion against my authority will never happen again. I am committed to you boys, and that means I must be in charge here. Whenever anyone is rebellious and difficult, it is the same as saying, 'Spank me.' I will never make the decision that it is time for you to be spanked. You will, by defying me. Please don't ask me to spank you again."

Alfred left the room and went to bed fighting back tears. As I walked through the boys' rooms there was not a peep. The boys and Alfred were calm, but I certainly was not. For most of that night I sat up trying to analyze what had taken place.

The next morning it seemed as though someone had sneaked in during the night and given me twelve different boys. The tension was gone and breakfast was a delight. The boys appeared to be calmer and actually relieved. Alfred was my best friend and could not do enough to help. The boys went off to school as if a battle had been completed and they had won.

I learned a great lesson that day. Children are very insecure when they do not know who is in charge or, worse yet, when the one in charge is an unpredictable, immature child like Alfred. Children want the security of structure and someone who will back it up. Children also want to get the negatives behind them as quickly as possible so they can feel forgiven and get on with life.

I could have escorted Alfred to his room instead of to my office that night. I probably would have had to do it a dozen times, however, and it still would not have proven to him who was in charge. I could have told him that for every time he refused to obey me he would be grounded one day, but he probably would have ended up the night being grounded for thirty days. That would mean paying a consequence for a whole month and spending the time feeling bitter and unforgiven. Worse than that, he would be spending a month feeling like a loser while he watched the other boys go on with life.

The most merciful form of punishment is the kind that is over quickly, allowing the child to feel forgiven. I could see the next morning that Alfred felt as clean and pure as snow. That was probably something he had not experienced for a long time. Alfred was even laughing at the breakfast table instead of trying to act like a tough guy.

Did Alfred ever need, or should I say "ask for," a spanking again? Of course he did. The crowning reassurance came to me nine years later when Alfred, then a young adult, pulled up to Sheridan House in his car with his twelve-year-old nephew.

"This is my sister's son, Bobby," Alfred said to us. "He needs to be here. Sheridan House needs to do for him what you did for me."

The message had gotten through to Alfred, even though we spent days dealing with his rebellious behavior. The manner in which we did it—establishing consistent rules, spanking for rebellion, and then forgiving—had proven to Alfred that we were committed to him and that we loved him.

The Most Important Book

Shortly after that night spent with Alfred, God sent me a message through a very godly woman. Mrs. Molly Sipple came to visit me at Sheridan House to see how the new director was doing. As we sat talking in my office, I noticed that this lady in her seventies was staring at all the books I had on my shelves. Finally, Mrs. Sipple asked me, "Which one of all your books do you feel is the most important book to help you in your work with these children?"

I leaned back in my chair and replied, "Oh, I don't know, Mrs. Sipple. Maybe Dobson, or Blos, or maybe even Shrader."

After a moment's pause she said to me, "How about the Bible? Have you ever searched that for answers on how to help these children?"

Embarrassed, I acknowledged to her that she was right, and we moved on to other subjects. But Mrs. Sipple's words had hit me square between the eyes, so after she had gone I decided to take a look at some of God's principles for dealing with children. After all, he ought to know. He created them. For me to ignore the Bible on the subject of discipline would be the same as if I had purchased a Chevrolet and tried to maintain it using a Maytag washing machine manual.

I began to search the Bible and found some very helpful advice. In Proverbs, God not only instructs us to spank, but he is very specific as to how to do it: "Folly is bound up in the heart of a child, but the rod of discipline will drive it far from him" (Proverbs 22:15). Not only does this verse say that parents should expect a child to challenge their authority, but also that God expects us to spank them.

In my opinion, this verse also indicates that we should not spank children with our hand. "The rod of correction" indicates some sort of implement other than a hand. My hand is too convenient; it is too easy to act impulsively or harshly with my hand. By reacting with the hand, a parent could wrongfully slap a child in the face. A wooden spoon or paddle, however, can only be used in the place God provided with padding. A wooden spoon is also something that a parent has to walk into the kitchen to get while he is thinking about the real purpose for the discipline about to take place. It is to instruct the child, not to relieve a parent's anger or frustration.

Spanking is for the child, to meet the child's needs and not the parent's. Does that mean that I must carry a wooden spoon with me to the grocery store? No, I do not, although I know some parents who do. Some implement is the ideal, but obviously a parent will not always have one when the child's behavior asks for a spanking. On those occasions I have used my hand on the bottom of my child.

Proverbs 13:24 says, "He who spares the rod hates his son, but he who loves him is careful to discipline him." "Sparing the rod" by not disciplining at all or by waiting until later is emotionally abusive to the child, as he must sit and anticipate the spanking. Parents must be prompt with the spanking and equally prompt with the love, forgiveness, and hugs.

Torrey's Test

When our first child, Torrey, began to crawl, I started to remove the things that I did not want her to touch. I thought by doing that I could relieve our home of conflicts between parent and child. Quickly, Rosemary and I realized that that was impossible. Just as we would move one thing out of Torrey's reach she would crawl over to another thing. We quickly saw the need to teach the concept of no. Moving everything out of her reach did not teach Torrey anything and it soon exhausted us. And understanding the word *no* is especially important outside of the home, at friends' houses, where things are not moved out of a child's reach.

One morning, right after Torrey had learned to walk, the whole family was sitting in our living room. Torrey had her spill-proof juice cup and Rosemary and I each had coffee. Rosemary had taught Torrey that she could put her juice cup on any table in the room with the exception of one very special Early American coffee table. She had established this one rule, and Rosemary had spanked Torrey in the past for disobeying it.

That morning, Rosemary got up and took our coffee cups into the kitchen for a refill. Just as she left the room Torrey decided she would check to see if Daddy was as committed to the rules as Mommy. She got up, waddled over to the table, and started to put her juice cup down on the coffee table.

To help her, I said, "No, no, Honey, please don't put your cup on that table."

Torrey stopped for a moment, turned to watch me, and plopped her cup right on the edge of the table. Then she smiled as if to say, "I know what Mommy would do if she were here. But what about you, Dad? What are you going to do?"

I almost looked into the kitchen to see how long it would be before Rosemary would be back. Coward that I was, I would have liked for her to handle Torrey's challenge. I did realize, however, that this defiance had been directed at me. I could have removed the table in question from the living room. But the challenge had very little to do with the table. It was my authority and ability to love Torrey and help her grow up as an obedient child that was being challenged.

I got up, walked into the kitchen, and got a wooden spoon. Returning to the living room, I gave my little daughter a swat on the bottom with the spoon. Then I nearly died. It was the first time that I had spanked her, and I suddenly realized what my dad had meant when he said, "Son, this hurts me more than it hurts you."

Nobody said it would be easy, but God did say it would be necessary. And then Torrey did something that amazed me. Crying, she reached up toward me for comfort. Me, the one who had just spanked her! I picked up my little daughter, held her, and tried to explain to her why she had just been spanked. I forgave her immediately, and in a few minutes she was down on the floor playing happily.

Torrey learned her lesson and did not put her cup back on the table, regardless of who was present. And I learned an even greater lesson. God again was right. Spanking is the most merciful response to rebellion. It enhances my child's self-esteem because it is so quickly over and life can go on.

I cannot stress enough, however, that after the child has been spanked, she must be forgiven, shown love, and even hugged. Some children may reject physical contact, and in that case a parent shouldn't force a hug. The parent's job, however, is to show the child that she is loved and forgiven. This final part of the spanking process is extremely important for the child's self-esteem. The behavior must be rejected—not the child.

13

MAINTAINING CONSISTENCY

Have you ever worked for two different bosses at the same time? One summer during college, I worked as a laborer for a small construction company. A foreman was my immediate boss, but the owner of the company would call me a couple of times a day to do errands. The owner, a loud, boisterous man, demanded that I drop everything to complete his errands. My foreman, in contrast, would let me know each morning what we were going to do that day and what I needed to accomplish on my own. He was never loud and seemed to control his frustrations quite well.

The foreman naturally expected me to complete a job when he left me alone. However, when the owner saw me working alone, he often would pull me off the foreman's job and put me on one of his own projects. When the foreman realized what had happened, he would be quietly furious and try to pull me off the owner's job.

Halfway through the summer, it got to the point of being ridiculous. I would get lectures from both of my bosses. "I don't care what he calls you over for," each would say. "You just stay right here and finish!" I knew they both liked me and that I was getting stretched in both directions for reasons that had nothing to do with me. Instead of talking to each other, they were pulling my body from place to place to communicate their frustrations.

One day the owner called out the window to me. "When you get a chance, Bob, I need you to come into the office and vacuum our new rugs."

I knew exactly what that meant. He would wait until I got started on a job for the foreman and then he would come to find me. Unfortunately, the foreman heard his request and decided to checkmate the owner—using me as his pawn.

That day there was a drag in the sewer line in the development we were building, and at the catch station there was a buildup of about six inches of sewage. My foreman handed me a set of waders, a small sledge hammer, and a chisel, and after we took the lid off, he sent me down to wade around and chisel the floor of the catch station.

The smell was terrible. Never in my life had I encountered a more disgusting job. I knew that it would probably take a "skunk" cologne to cover this odor. But the full extent of the foreman's wiles didn't dawn on me until I heard the owner calling for me.

"He's down here," the foreman shouted back.

The owner said, "Well, send him up here."

The foreman replied, "He's pretty busy with a real messy job."

"I don't care what he's doing; send him right now!" the owner shouted.

Well, you can imagine the smile on my foreman's face when he said, "You heard the man, Bob. He wants you in the office immediately."

I didn't know quite how badly I stank until I stepped into that office. The owner backed away, the smile of victory fading quickly from his face and replaced by storm clouds of fury.

I could see I was about to get the lecture that had been brewing all summer, so I quickly said, "I'm leaving. If you want me to keep working here, I need to talk to you and the foreman together. Otherwise I'll pick up my last check tonight."

Uncoordinated Parents

Jesus once said, "No servant can serve two masters" (Luke 16:13). I discovered that truth in my summer job. I could not work for two bosses who handed down conflicting orders.

Children also cannot function properly when their parents give them conflicting signals. Because their parents haven't taken the first and most basic step in the family structure—deciding the approach they are going to take with their children—children are left confused. The saddest part about an uncoordinated approach to parenting is that the child is the loser. Never being quite sure which parent's rules are in effect, he can't feel secure or confident about how to respond.

For parents to work together, they need to set up "staff meetings" between themselves. There they can decide on the rules that will be upheld consistently by both parents.

Peter Olsen, a ten-year-old resident at Sheridan House, illustrates this need for consistency. His parents took him for counseling because he seemed withdrawn and moody. Such behavior could be the outward manifestation of many different problems. Before long, however, we saw that it was not so much Peter but the parents who needed help.

Mr. and Mrs. Olsen had trouble communicating with

each other. They were not even able to talk about their marriage, much less about how Peter should be raised. In addition, each parent had a set opinion about the rules that Peter should live by, and those rules were more important than anything else, including Peter's happiness.

Mr. Olsen felt that Peter should do his chores before he did anything else on Saturday. Mrs. Olsen did not feel that her husband's rule was important, so she did not enforce it. Peter would be sitting in front of the television watching cartoons when his dad would walk into the room and explode. "I thought I told you to clean your room and make your bed before you watched cartoons!"

"But Mom said—" Peter would attempt to reply.

"I don't care *what* your mom said. I told you to do your chores first," Peter's dad would yell. "Now, get up, turn off the television, and get at it! And for disobeying me, you will have one more chore added to your list this morning."

Mrs. Olsen, listening in the kitchen, would sneak into Peter's room to soften the blow. She helped him do his chores, thinking it would make things better for Peter. Unfortunately for Peter it only made things worse. His dad became even more frustrated and angry.

Emotionally, Peter was being pulled apart by his two parents because they would not sit down and develop a consistent plan for their home. Peter, stuck in a no-win situation, had to watch his step every minute to make sure he wouldn't break someone's rules.

This is a relatively common situation. The child is caught in the middle of two parents who use him to get at each other. As one tries to tone down or subvert the authority of the other, the more structured parent becomes even more frustrated and overreacts with consequences that are much too severe. The child is pulled in two different directions and begins to feel that he just cannot please either parent.

Rules must be consistently upheld by both parents. The fact that one parent may be home and in charge at one particular time and the other parent at another time should have no bearing on whether a rule is in effect or not. If the structure is consistently and objectively adhered to, the child quickly learns that he is fighting against a rule and not against a parent.

God has given us rules to live by because he loves us. So as not to cause us confusion, he has made the rules consistent, universal, and unchanging. Thus I really don't break one of God's *rules* when I choose to sin. Instead, I break *myself* up against God's rules.

Just as God's love for me has caused him to be perfectly consistent, so must my love for my child cause me and my spouse to set a consistent policy. The child needs an environment he can understand and deal with, and in which he can be creative. And both parent and child need to avoid the constant frustration that inconsistency creates.

Now I Can Really Love My Child

Peter's parents spent a long time working on their own communication difficulties and finally got to a point where they could develop a consistent plan for Peter. They learned the very significant fact that parents may be a little too lenient or a little too strict, but it is being *consistent* in what they are doing that is important.

Mr. and Mrs. Olsen were then able to separate the child from his behavior. It was the bad or unacceptable behavior they needed to punish—not the child. Often parents take it personally when a child disobeys. They don't see it for the disobedience it is but think, *Why is he doing this to me?* In reality, the child is not doing anything to anybody but himself, and a self-pitying attitude like the above will only make the parent and child adversaries. A parent should deal with the behavior and be very careful not to go further by withdrawing love at the same time.

Discipline the behavior and love the child. In her book, *It's My Turn*, Ruth Graham talks about disciplining her rebellious little boy, Franklin. They were almost at war with each other when in desperation she prayed for God's guidance. God's answer? Love Franklin even more. Deal with the behavior, but love the child outwardly, physically, and verbally.

Many parents complain that their child makes it difficult for them to love her, for she doesn't *do* anything to be loved for. But *doing* is not the point. If the parents deal consistently with the behavior, then they can and should love their child, *just because she is theirs*.

I saw Mr. and Mrs. Olsen in a store not long ago and asked them how things were progressing at home with Peter. Mr. Olsen responded in a beautiful way. "We are working together now as parents, and you know what? Now I can really love my child."

This is not a new philosophy of discipline. As a matter of fact, it is exactly the way our Lord and Father deals with us. God hates our sin, but he loves us with a love more powerful than we could ever comprehend. Love, and the forgiveness that comes along with it, is perhaps the most important ingredient of discipline. Our heavenly Father has us refer to him as Father to show us that as he loves and forgives us, we too as parents must love and forgive our own children.

PART IV

What Else Do I Need to Teach My Child?

14

ADOPTING A PHILOSOPHY
OF LIFE

Parents constantly ask, "Why do teenagers live just for the moment? Why don't they work hard for their future?"

I used to ask the same questions. How could you teach children to plan for the future? How did you show them that there was more to life than satisfying their immediate desires? A fourteen-year-old boy named Barry Ellis showed me the answer to this question.

The Ellis family had come to me for counseling because it was falling apart. No one was happy, and they could not seem to talk to each other about it. Communication had shut down as each family member went his or her own separate way. Barry and his sister had once done fairly well in school and had participated happily in family activities. But now they had grown sullen and were getting very poor grades.

To rectify the situation, Mr. and Mrs. Ellis had tried church for a while, then camping on weekends for six months or so. Now Mr. Ellis was more concerned with golf on Sundays, unless of course there were football games on television to watch instead.

One night as I was counseling the family, Mr. Ellis began to say, "I believe—"

"What *do* you believe in, Dad?" Barry interrupted.

Mr. Ellis, taken aback, just looked at him.

"We used to believe that camping together and being

together was important," Barry said. "Before that, we believed, or at least we were told we believed, that church was important. Does our family believe in anything?" Frustration and hurt were written all over Barry's face.

The room was silent for at least thirty seconds. Mr. Ellis had no answer. He really did not know what he believed was significant in life, and without knowing it himself, he could not teach it to his family.

We all adopt and live by a philosophy of life. Mr. Ellis did not know that he had established a philosophy of life to live by, but indeed he had. His philosophy was to live for today, try this road and then try that one. His life-style said to his son Barry that there is really nothing worth living for in the future so you had better have fun today.

Why do young people seem so despondent about the future? Why do so many of them act as if they are unwilling to work hard today for tomorrow's goals? Why do so many adolescents seem to reject their parents' ideals? It is not an attitude that has originated with them. As I mentioned before, children are trained first of all by the example that the parents set for them. Children unconsciously scrutinize their parents to find out what their philosophy of life is. Unfortunately, many parents are not teaching or exemplifying a worthy philosophy of life to their children.

By living for the next new car, the bigger house, the next raise, or any other material or experiential happening, we are actually teaching children that life is to be lived for what we can get out of it *now*—or at least as quickly as possible. This philosophy of life says to a child, "There's really nothing more in life than the pleasures you can feel or the power you can gain. It's every man for himself."

How many children have lived in a home where one

parent has thrown a longtime marriage commitment out of the window for the momentary pleasure of an extra-marital affair? Or how many children are raised to believe that there is absolutely nothing after death? If a child believes he has come from nothing, for no real purpose, and that he will return to dust, he will feel he is cheating himself not to live solely for the joy and fun of each moment. After all, according to this philosophy of life, he could return to dust at any moment. With that hanging over his head, a child believes it is foolish to invest in tomorrow.

A child's parents must establish and set an example of a worthy philosophy of life. If the child is not aware of the precious security of life after death, then it is little wonder many children are despondent and have low self-esteem, for children need a worthy philosophy of life to which they can cling.

What Is a Philosophy of Life?

Simply put, a philosophy of life is what a person believes in. It is the core or central idea that we come back to when we make decisions. If a person's particular philosophy of life is to keep his body pure, then as he goes through life he will base many of his decisions on this. When offered cigarettes or drugs, he will reject them because they go against his philosophy of life. When asked if he wants to play tennis, he may accept because it will be good for his body.

As we go through life, we face many difficult decisions. Our philosophy of life—what we stand for, believe in, or want—is at the core of our being, and if it is strong, it will have a very significant impact on the decisions we make.

But if it is not a God-honoring philosophy, it can cause us great pain.

It is extremely important that children are taught a philosophy of life that answers the crucial questions: Who am I? What do I believe? Am I of any value? Where am I going when I die? A philosophy of life that teaches a child to live for pleasure or strive for wealth does not answer these most crucial questions.

Other things help to develop a child's self-esteem; for example, her parents' love and understanding. However, the greatest determining factor in the development of a child's self-esteem is her philosophy of life.

The Only Worthy Philosophy of Life

When Tim was a boy, his father was an executive with a major corporation. The family lived very comfortably and Tim was taught, "If you want something in life, Son, you have to work for it." Tim's dad and mom were strong, moral people, and Tim knew he could look to his parents, especially his dad, for strength. In fact, Tim all but worshiped his father, and his philosophy of life came to be, "I want to be just like my dad—strong, moral, and relentless in my pursuit of life."

Perhaps it was a good philosophy of life, or at least better than some of the other options. However, it certainly was not a worthy philosophy of life to build an entire life on.

When Tim became a teenager, tragedy struck his home. His mother died unexpectedly due to an illness. Naturally, Tim turned to his dad for strength. After all, the boy's philosophy of life had been "Cling to Dad; he can do anything. He can make me happy again." Unfortunately, his dad had no strength to offer. Instead, his father fell apart and spent months, even years, in mourning.

Tim could barely explain which of the two events were more shocking to him, his mother's death or his father's collapse. His dad had never shown weakness before. The philosophy of life that Tim had been able to cling to for direction—worshiping his dad and his strength—vanished. With it vanished his self-esteem. He no longer believed in anything that gave him a direction in life.

For the next several years, Tim searched for something new to believe in. First he tried to become the best athlete he could possibly be. For a while this became the very core of his being, and his self-esteem vacillated according to how well he performed. If he had a good game, Tim felt valuable and good about himself. If his game went badly, Tim hated himself. Tim had fallen into the trap of basing his self-esteem on his performance.

Next Tim pursued educational goals. He completed college, and that goal over, he looked for something new to believe in. Everyone else seemed to work toward financial success, so he did that for a time. But he realized that money was not the answer either. He became depressed and began to ask himself, *Is this all there is?*

With self-esteem at an all-time low, Tim was finally told about a worthy philosophy of life. He learned that the only thing in life he could truly believe in and count on is the God who created him. He learned that he, like everyone else, had sinned, and was in need of a savior. Searching for acceptance for who he was, rather than what he could do, Tim discovered a God who loved him so much that he sent his only Son, Jesus Christ, to die on the cross for him.

Tim began to develop a new philosophy of life. For the first time, he realized that he was loved in spite of his inadequacies, and it was a total, unconditional love. This new love that he had for Christ was also a very personal love. Finally Tim could worship someone who would never collapse or let him down.

Not only did Tim have a person to cling to, he also had a new philosophy of life he could consult for direction. Now when he made decisions, he could look to the Bible for long-term, consistent answers. Whether he made decisions about money, his sex life, his marriage, or anything else, his new philosophy of life could be counted upon to help him. Finally, Tim had a philosophy of life that could last a lifetime and beyond!

In order for children to feel truly valuable, they must be pointed toward a central belief in something that says, "You are personally precious and valuable." A child must be shown that there is something worth believing in and building a life on, something even more loving and consistent than the parent himself.

In the early chapters of this book we talked about answering the question "Whom do I belong to?" The child who can answer that question, "I belong to God," is bound to feel valuable. Parents, therefore, can do no greater thing for their children's self-esteem than to show them Christ as the foundation for their philosophy of life.

15

LEARNING TO BE CONFIDENT
WITH MONEY

"Mom, can I have some money?" This was almost a daily request from Daniel. Each time he asked, his parents asked what he was going to use it for, determined if they could afford to give him a few dollars at that particular time, and decided whether he should have the money or not. If for some reason Mr. and Mrs. Jackson could not give Daniel the money, an argument would ensue and everyone would feel bad about it. He would beg, cajole, cry, and try to make them feel guilty.

Daniel had absolutely no responsibility with money and was learning nothing about saving. Sometimes he even felt guilty about the way he had to try to manipulate his parents to get pocket money.

Unfortunately, Daniel's situation is a common one. When parents accept sole responsibility for handling their children's money, they actually *encourage* their children to manipulate them for money. Frustrated by an inconsistent system, children will whine and cry and manipulate their parents for money. This pattern, however, only increases fighting between parent and child and damages a child's self-esteem.

A child needs to learn through experience that he is capable of handling money, and then his self-esteem will grow as well. Self-esteem grows when a child works *with* his parents' system rather than against it.

When I asked Mr. and Mrs. Jackson why they did not give Daniel a weekly allowance, they gave me the classic excuse: "We really can't afford to give him an allowance." I told them that they could not afford *not* to—for two reasons.

First, in the long run, giving an allowance is more economical than giving haphazard amounts. If parents were ever to keep track of the money they haphazardly distribute to their child, they would be shocked. One week a parent may be low on funds so he might say to the child, "This is all I have to give you for now," or even, "I'm sorry, I wish I could give you some money this weekend, but I can't." The following week, however, the parent very likely will attempt to compensate for the previous week by giving the child more money to spend than the family can really afford. Throughout the year this up-and-down approach would probably add up to a higher total than a weekly allowance would have. A weekly allowance can be budgeted and handled in an objective manner. The other approach—handing out money on demand—is purely subjective as far as the child sees it.

Second, a child can learn a lot about personal discipline and responsibility through handling money. I learned that lesson on a vacation one year in the mountains of North Carolina. My daughter, Torrey, was only four years old at the time, and we were spending three weeks in a cabin loaned to us by a friend. Torrey had just begun receiving an allowance of one dollar a week at home, but she had no money with her on vacation. Each morning after breakfast, our family got into the car and drove around the mountains, visiting the various shops.

The first morning we visited a store Torrey looked up at me and said, "Will you buy this for me, Daddy?" It was a little stuffed bear placed conveniently at child level. I picked it up and bought it for her. Torrey loved her new bear—for about an hour. Then as we went into other stores all I heard for the rest of the morning was "Buy me this, Daddy" and "Buy me that, Daddy."

Inadvertently I had set up a system that encouraged Torrey to ask and keep asking until she finally got something. By the end of the day we were both exhausted. She felt discouraged and depressed because she had been a little beggar all day and received numerous lectures and glares from me. And I felt depressed because this was not the kind of father I wanted to be. I had looked forward to spending a happy three weeks with Torrey. I knew, however, that something had to change if we were going to continue visiting the mountain shops.

Later that evening after the children were in bed, my wife and I discussed the day's happenings. I asked Rosemary, "How do you take Torrey into the stores back home and keep your sanity?"

"Before she got an allowance," my wife replied, "I would let her know before we even went into a store if I was going to give her spending money. That way she would not beg for everything she saw, but spend her time deciding what she wanted. For instance, before we went to the grocery store I would tell her, 'I have a quarter for you to have, honey. You may buy gum, or a cookie from the bakery, or whatever you want. In fact, you can even save it for later.' I think we should tell Torrey that since it's vacation she can have a dollar each morning to spend as she wishes."

The next morning the announcement was made. "Torrey," I said, "yesterday you and I argued in almost every store we were in, and I feel bad about that. In fact, I don't want to do that anymore, so your mom and I have decided that since this is vacation and we have extra money to spend, we're going to give you some money for your very own. Each morning I will give you one dollar and you can spend it as you wish. Here is your dollar for today."

Shortly after that discussion, we all packed into the car and drove off down the mountain to visit some new shops. As we walked into the first shop, Torrey saw a toy and said, as usual, "Will you buy me this little horse, Daddy?" I had to remind her that she now had her own money to spend.

It was interesting how quickly she adapted to a new line of questions. "How much does this cost, Daddy?" Finally, Torrey found an item that she could afford, and I knew that was the only reason she wanted it. It was all I could do to bite my tongue and let her buy it. It was a piece of junk, but part of the deal was to give her some purchasing freedom with her own money. And she was amazingly proud of this purchase. If she saw anyone we knew that day she was quick to tell them, "I bought this with my own money." Later on that day Torrey did ask once if she could have something, to which Rosemary replied, "Do you have any money left, honey?" Torrey caught on very quickly, and the day went remarkably well.

This little plan revolutionized the rest of our vacation, and it all culminated with an event that had a strong impact on Torrey's self-esteem. One day, in the middle of our stay in the mountains, Torrey saw a plastic pony that she wanted very badly. When she asked me how much it was, I showed her that the price was $4.50—much more than her dollar. I could see that she wanted this horse, so we went out and sat on a bench in front of the shop to discuss it.

All of a sudden I saw her little face light up. I knew what was coming. Looking at me beseechingly she said, "Daddy, will you lend me the extra money and just not give me any more dollars until I've paid you back?"

My heart ached, but I said no. "Honey, you can save your money for four more days, and that will give you enough money to buy it." After the talk, Torrey was upset. She walked back into the shop only to buy the first junky toy she saw.

Torrey obviously spent time that day thinking about how dissatisfied she was with herself and her purchase. Before dinner she came out onto the porch where I was reading and said, "Daddy, I want to save my money for that horse." I was very gratified by her decision, but the next few days were tough. Torrey walked through the stores looking at the items longingly and knowing that she had the money in her purse. Many times I wanted to say, "Go ahead and spend your money; I'll buy your horse for you." But by doing that, I would have been meeting my own immediate need instead of training Torrey to save toward the future.

Five days went by. Finally the day arrived when Torrey could buy her pony. Immediately after breakfast, we went back to the store, and Torrey selected a pony. She paid for the toy, then walked out of the shop holding it next to her heart. I could not believe how proud she looked!

We all had learned a great lesson. By making Torrey responsible for a specific and regular amount of money, we stopped the begging and arguing that can be so counterproductive to a child's self-esteem. When we allowed her the privilege of saving toward something she wanted, instead of simply buying it for her, we allowed her a chance to feel like she accomplished something.

Torrey got two things with her purchase that day. Not only did she get the pony she had saved for, but she also got to taste the feeling of accomplishment and personal worth.

It has been years since then, and there is only one remnant from that vacation. In her closet Torrey still has that little $4.50 pony. Special as it was, I don't really believe it is nice enough to have been saved that long. I think that somewhere deep inside her that pony has come to represent a feeling of accomplishment.

Allowance

Children should be given a specific amount of money to spend and it should be just that—theirs to spend. When I was a boy, my dad handed out allowances each Friday evening when he got home. If we happened to go out that evening and I got near a store that sold baseball cards, very likely that would be it for my allowance! I would come out of the store with three packs of cards in my hand, three pieces of baseball-card gum in my mouth, and no more money in my pocket. The next day if I wanted to go roller skating and went to my dad to borrow some money, he would always have the same response, "Bob, I am not a savings and loan institution."

I was given an allowance each Friday evening like clockwork, but that was it until the next Friday evening. I was the one responsible for making it last. I was the one responsible for having enough money to make it through the week. There were many times when I failed and spent all of my money before the week was out, but my dad always maintained his integrity in this allowance program. If I spent it, I went without.

At times I got upset with my dad for not advancing me money until the next week. It never changed his mind, though. To teach me financial responsibility, my dad stood by one important concept: It was better for me to fail at handling a few dollars at a young age than to fail at handling thousands of dollars as an adult. He withstood my anger when he wouldn't lend me money so that I might be saved from financial catastrophes as an adult. Today I am very grateful for this lesson.

Tithing

Giving children a quarter each Sunday to put into an offering plate teaches them very little about the concept of tithing. It also robs them of the privilege of feeling they are contributing toward God's work.

I did not become a Christian until early adulthood, so the concept of tithing was new to me. It was also incredibly difficult for me to do. Finally, after much soul-searching, I realized that tithing was not an option but a command. God does not need my money. It is I who need to give him my money as a way of reminding myself that he takes priority. It is not my money, but rather my love and obedience that the tithe represents.

Because I had such a difficult time with tithing, I wanted to be sure that my children wouldn't have such a difficult time learning this practice. To teach our children to tithe, then, we gave them an allowance. When Torrey was five, we gave her an allowance of one dollar in ten dimes so that she could easily figure out what a tenth was. We also gave her her own offering envelopes to use. Very quickly she understood the joy of giving to God. Often she would put more than one dime into the offering envelope and be very proud of it.

Allowance and Chores

Experts disagree over whether allowance should be connected to the completion of household chores. Many experts believe that a child should not receive an allowance unless she does something to earn it. Some believe that a young child should be paid by the chore so as to teach a child to work for her money.

I disagree with this way of handling the child's allowance. I do not think a child should be paid for doing his share of the chores. Chores are a contribution to the welfare of the home. As a father, I do not get an extra bonus for doing my chore of cutting the lawn. Nor should children get paid for their chores, for they are working as part of the family team.

When they become teenagers, children who are paid to do chores around the house often stop doing their chores. After all, they can make more money elsewhere in a part-time job. Children, therefore, should be taught that chores are done for the good of the family, not for the money.

Young children should be given an allowance and chores, but the two should not be contingent on each other. Teenagers should be given chores, but they may not need an allowance when they begin to make money on their own. Until that point, however, an allowance is the only tool that a parent can use to teach a child how to handle money responsibly.

16

UNDERSTANDING SEX
AT AN EARLY AGE

"Mommy, how did baby John get out of your tummy?" asked five-year-old Judy.

"I'll tell you when you are a little older, honey," her mother replied.

"Dad, what is this?" four-year-old Peyton asked, pointing to his penis.

"Son, that's something you don't ask questions about," Peyton's dad said.

"Does Mommy have one, Dad?"

"Peyton!" his dad warned. End of conversation—maybe for life.

As children grow and discover more and more of the wonders of their world, they have a need for definitions. "What is this?" or "How does that work?" are natural questions, and parents usually answer those questions readily—unless they are questions about sex. Unfortunately, when young children ask about sex, they often receive evasive or harsh responses, and they are made to feel guilty for asking.

Anna was a typical five-year-old with an inquisitive mind and a desire to search for answers. One morning she asked her father, "What does my heart do, Daddy?"

Her father, Jim, responded, "It pumps the blood through your body, honey."

"How does it do that, Daddy? Is it made of metal?" Anna persisted.

When Jim realized that he did not have the remotest idea how to answer Anna, he got out the encyclopedia to show her pictures while he talked. Before long Anna had all the information she wanted.

Anna felt good about being able to go to her father with questions. Jim also felt good as he put the encyclopedia back. He knew almost nothing about how the heart functioned, and yet he was able to find the necessary information and help his daughter. He told his daughter, "If you have any more questions, honey, come on back and we'll find the answers together in the encyclopedia."

Anna found that her dad kept his promise. She came to him with questions about space shuttles, broken bones, tadpoles, and many other things. Dad became an amazing resource person as they searched the encyclopedia together. Then one day Anna made a terrible mistake. She was not sure how it happened or why it happened. It just did.

Anna began the conversation with her usual opener, "Daddy, I have another question for you." Jim, having come to enjoy his newfound role of instructor, put his newspaper down and asked, "What would you like to know about, honey?"

"What is a penis, Dad?"

Total silence. A cloud seemed to come over Jim's face. "Who told you that word, Anna?"

Anna, feeling the sudden coldness, said hesitantly, "I heard Mommy tell Billy to wash his penis. What is a penis?"

"It's something Billy has and you don't, so don't worry about it."

"Why don't I have one? Which encyclopedia should I

get, Daddy?" Anna thought asking questions might put her dad back into a good mood. In the past her interest in things had always pleased him. But not this time.

"That is something you do not need to know about, Anna, so don't ask me any more questions." Jim picked up his paper and hid behind it.

Over the next twelve months or so, a pattern developed. Jim was more than available to help Anna learn about anything she desired—anything, that is, except how babies are born, or sexual anatomy. Those kinds of questions were met with a frown and made Anna feel as if she were a bad girl for wanting to know the answers to such questions.

Jim's philosophy of sex education was "If she doesn't know about it, it can't get her into trouble." He did not realize the damage that he was doing to his daughter's self-esteem and to their future relationship. She was being made to feel guilty or even dirty for having such questions about herself. *Maybe there is something wrong with me, or maybe I'm a bad girl for wanting to know the answers to these questions. Could parts of my body be good and other parts be bad?* she wondered.

It was a confusing area for Anna, and she became insecure about it. Unfortunately, it could not be cleared up, because her father had made it quite clear that those kinds of questions were bad. If Anna wanted to learn about her sexuality, she knew she would have to go someplace other than home.

Jim's attitude did more than stifle the questions of a little girl; they blockaded the questions of a young teenager. The topics of sexual development or reproduction became a taboo between the two of them. Even when Anna became an adolescent, Jim could not bring up the subject. After much frustration he just gave up, bought a book on sex education, and left it on his daughter's bed. Tragically, it was too late. Anna had already been seeking information about her sexuality elsewhere. She had already learned long ago that she could discuss anything in the world with her dad, except one of life's most special topics: what it was to be a godly woman in the area of her sexuality.

Sex Education That Promotes Self-Esteem

When Laury was born, her parents went to the Christian bookstore to get information on parenting. Almost as an afterthought, Laury's dad, Mike, purchased a book on sex education. He didn't think he would need it until Laury was an adolescent, at which time he would refer to it to teach her about sex.

One night, however, Mike happened to pick up the book about sex education and begin to read. He was interested to discover that sex education begins already at a young age. He learned that young children have a natural interest in the physical difference between boys and girls, how babies are made, and how they get out of the mother's tummy. When young children innocently and inquisitively ask questions about sexuality, parents should see these questions for what they are, innocent curiosity, and answer them simply and clearly, with as much information as the child desires. Clear answers will help the children feel good about their sexuality, and more important, will keep the lines of communication open on the topic of sexual development.

Although Mike was shocked by the bluntness of the author's suggestions, he found himself agreeing with the book's premise: When a child asks questions, answer them. So when he was put to the test, he knew what to do.

That day came when Laury was three. In the shower with Mike, she suddenly pointed and asked, "What's that, Daddy?"

Mike had several decisions to make at this point. Should he respond to the question or simply ignore it? If he responded to her question, should he give his sexual anatomy a cute label or should he teach her the proper word? In a flash he realized that one label was no different than another to her, so he might as well teach her the correct word. After all, Laury did not have hang-ups about labels yet. To her, an elbow or a penis were both simply names for parts of the body.

Mike responded to his daughter's question in a matter-of-fact manner, telling her that it was called a penis. Laury asked several more questions, and he answered them as accurately as he could. With her questions answered to her satisfaction, Laury went back to playing on the shower room floor with her toys.

Mike learned several things from that experience. He realized that questions about sex were easier to answer than he thought they would be because to Laury they were just matter-of-fact inquiries. He also learned that the ideal time to teach children about their sexual anatomy is when they are doing the asking. It becomes more and more difficult to begin this topic of discussion the older a child gets. Mike also realized that his daughter had reached the age at which he should no longer have her in the shower with him. When a child gets to the age where he or she is noticing the difference between the sexes, it is probably time to stop showering with the parent of the opposite sex.

As Laury grew older she asked her mom and dad many more questions, and they worked very hard to answer Laury's questions about reproduction. When these questions got more and more complex, they went back to the Christian bookstore and together with Laury purchased books that would help answer her questions. By the time Laury was seven years old, she knew exactly how babies were conceived, how they were born, and all the proper labels. To her this knowledge was no big deal. It was simply a fact of life like anything else pertaining to her body and her health.

Laury learned that all the parts of her body were good parts, made by God, and even those thought unmentionable were good parts, too. She also grew to see that her body and its functions were truly a miracle, that she was wonderfully made.

Laury felt good about herself and her sexuality. She knew that she could be free and open with her parents about sex, for they were always available to her for discussion and questions and nobody seemed to be embarrassed.

This openness in the early stages of Laury's life helped enhance her self-esteem and left good, guilt-free feelings about her body as a child. It also helped her tremendously later on in life. Since Laury's parents dealt with the discussion of anatomy when Laury was a young child, it left the rest of her childhood available for them to teach her how to handle her sexuality as a teenager. They talked with her about God's plan for sex in marriage and helped her develop a healthy plan of action for her teen years.

Her parents' openness about sex has benefited Laury, especially in her married life. As she went through the often difficult process of learning and growing with her husband sexually, she used her good attitude about her sexuality to help her talk about it with her husband. Secure in her own sexuality, she could learn from her husband and then risk teaching him about her needs.

Sex education that is not open and informative can hurt a child's self-esteem and later on plague his or her marriage, for unanswered questions lead only to insecurities. In contrast, showing openness and love when children ask questions helps them feel more secure about learning about themselves and their environment. They can then feel free to ask about how God would have them behave.

17

PERMITTING CHILDREN
TO MAKE MISTAKES

Dear Mom:

    I am sad to be writing this note to you and leaving it this way, but I just had to. Living at home is driving me crazy. I can't stand the way you constantly have to interfere in everything I try to do. It has gotten to the point where I don't even know if I can do anything. Every time I start to do something you step in and finish it for me.

    I tried to explain this to you last night, but every time I started talking you finished all my sentences for me and then tried to explain how I "really" felt. I saw that it was hopeless and have decided to leave for a while to try and think things through. I'll call and I love you.

> Your son,
> Jimmy

    Fifteen-year-old Jimmy Grogan was fed up with his mother. Mrs. Grogan was the kind of person who thought she had to see to it that her son succeeded at everything. Hovering over him, she never allowed him to do anything on his own. She dictated how he should do everything from chores, to homework, to conversations.

    Finally Jimmy and Mrs. Grogan met in my office to vent their frustration. Jimmy said, "Mom, I can't do anything without you interfering. If you hear me brushing my teeth, you come down the hall to tell me how to do it better."

"I just want you to benefit from all that I've learned," Mrs. Grogan said. "I don't want you to have to go through all the failures I've been through. It's just because I love you."

Mrs. Grogan did not want her son to fail, yet she was not letting him win at anything either. In order for children to feel good about themselves, they must feel that they can stand on their own, without their parent's help. Their self-esteem is enhanced when they learn to do more and more, but that same self-esteem is squelched when a parent continually denies a child the opportunity to learn by trial and error. There are few greater feelings than that of trying and trying and finally succeeding at something. Through trial and error, children slowly begin to feel competent. They think, *I'm not as stupid as I thought. Let me try something, and pretty soon I'll figure it out all right.* Their self-esteem is enhanced tremendously as they learn to use their own mind and God-given talents.

"I Can Do It"

One Sunday morning I knelt down to tie my three-and-a-half-year-old's shoes, and he said those magic words of independence: "I can do it, Daddy."

I knew Robey could not tie his shoes properly and we were on the verge of being late. There are few things I dislike more than being late. More than once I was tempted to push his fat little hands away and tie his shoes properly. But he sat bent over his shoes, working at those strings for all he was worth. I gritted my teeth and sat down with one eye on my watch. Finally, after an eternity (probably two or three minutes), Robey stood up and said, "Look, Daddy!"

His shoes were not even close to being tied properly, but he certainly thought they were. I could have untied them and started over, but he looked so proud that I simply said, "Good job, Robey, I'm proud of you."

Obviously, a parent does not want to compliment a child for a job poorly done. Doing this can give him a false sense of what is a good job and what is inadequate. Many children know that anyway, and can become frustrated at receiving compliments they know they do not deserve. A child can be complimented or encouraged for his effort, however, as in the case with Robey and his shoelaces.

Whenever anyone stopped to talk with us at church that morning Robey announced, "Look, I tied my shoes today." It was not necessarily what he had done that he was proud of. Robey was proud that it was *his* job; *he* had done it. If I had retied his shoes for him so that he would look perfect, with my help, I doubt if he would have said or felt anything. I cannot imagine Robey saying, "Look at the great tying job my dad did. I tried to do it, but I goofed up so my dad fixed it."

No, in a child's eyes, a parent can do just about everything. There is no reason for a parent to receive acclaim for such tasks. The child, however, is different in his own estimation. He is trying to become accomplished in almost every skill that adults take for granted. To think that I almost robbed my child of that great feeling of accomplishment! As parents, our attempts to love and help our children often do more harm than good. Their self-esteem needs, even demands, that they begin to develop as individuals.

The wise parent gives children challenges and lets them figure them out on their own. When you allow your children to grow and develop, you will have children who feel good about themselves and their family. They will not have to constantly assert their independence by acting rebellious.

Whereas Mrs. Grogan erred by dominating Jimmy's life, other parents err when they take a completely hands-off approach. Parents should not overwhelm their children with responsibilities they are not able to handle. Independence does not happen overnight but is a gradual process, with differing degrees of supervision required along the way. A good way to determine a child's abilities is to consult books on child development to see what the typical child can handle at various stages, always remembering that children develop at different rates. Parents should give children enough responsibility and independence to challenge them, but not so much that they become frustrated.

The Overprotective Christian Parent

"We just didn't want Brenda to make any mistakes that would mar her for life," said Mr. and Mrs. Michaels. So they kept Brenda busy in church activities, sent her to Christian schools, and allowed her to date only Christians. They made all her social decisions for her.

Then Brenda left home to attend a private Christian college, going from an environment where she made no decisions whatsoever to a college where she had to make all her own social decisions. Without any decision-making practice at all, Brenda was now supposed to make the right choices.

As anyone can imagine, this young girl failed dismally. Lacking confidence in her ability to make the right decisions, she simply went with the crowd. Her parents' over-protection had not really protected her at all. This protection may have made the parents feel secure while

Brenda was living at home, but it had a negative impact on her own self-esteem. She felt unable to make the right choices because she had never been allowed to stand on her own and make any choices before.

Mrs. Michael's lament was, "We just didn't want our child to make any mistakes that would mar her for life." But the biggest mistake had been theirs when they did not allow Brenda to make her own decisions about her social life.

Adolescents will make mistakes when they are allowed to decide for themselves about some of the issues they face. Yet those mistakes and failures are all part of the growing-up process.

I once talked to a pastor friend about his teenage daughter. I had heard that he was allowing her to set her own curfew in her senior year, and I asked him about it.

"This kind of decision is not new for Linda," my friend said. "My wife and I have slowly been putting these decisions in her lap and holding her responsible for them. This had been difficult for me personally, because as a pastor I know that if she makes some bad choices it could have a detrimental impact on my ministry. But we decided that her need to learn how to make wise and godly decisions is more important than my needs at this point.

"As we put more and more responsibility on Linda's shoulders, we have seen her self-esteem grow. Linda has begun to feel more confident in her ability to stand on her own."

"How does she set her own curfew?" I asked.

"Instead of setting a specific time that Linda is to be home we told her that she would have to decide for herself as each particular event or date comes up. Before she leaves she says, 'I'm going out to such and such a place and I'll be home before such and such a time.' I then hold her accountable for whatever time she tells us. Sure, it's rough for me to watch my little girl go out the door. But that's just it. She isn't a little girl anymore. I know that in just a few short months she will be leaving us. I will no longer be around to help her with decisions. Linda will be on her own at college."

This father then made a statement that I will never forget. "Many of the decisions Linda makes now will have a major impact on her future and her self-esteem. She will certainly fail in some areas and make the wrong decisions. As painful as it is for us, as loving parents, we are allowing her the opportunity to make those decisions while she is still at home. I would rather that my child fail in a decision and come back that night to a home and family that loves her than fail and return to an empty dormitory room."

No one wants her child to fail. We would all like to protect our children from failure and bad decisions, but it is just not possible. Everyone who is given an opportunity to make personal decisions makes the wrong ones from time to time. To attempt to protect a child from making bad decisions is only to postpone failure until the child is out of the house. But failure that occurs while a child is still at home can be a great learning experience and self-esteem booster, as she sees she is still loved and valued for who she is rather than for what she does.

In addition, children who experience failure while they are at home have the advantage of the presence of loving parents who will help them discuss what they have done. When children have parents who listen and gently guide them, they learn not only how to make better decisions, but also that their parents are available to listen and give direction.

Learning through failing also encourages children to try harder. Their self-esteem is enhanced as they build their confidence in their ability to be responsible for their own decisions.

A home that permits a child the freedom to make decisions and to fail is a home that is allowing a child to grow, that is working to meet the child's needs rather than those of the parents. The home that never allows a child the opportunity to decide anything for himself is a home that is meeting the needs of the parents rather than those of the child.

The process of a child's emancipation begins early, when she tries to feed herself or to walk alone. As a first grader she chooses for herself the clothes she'll wear. And as a teenager, she begins to make decisions about her social life. In each stage of her life, she is given various tasks to do, and the parents get out of the way. She is not given total freedom, but she is slowly given more and more opportunities to make her own decisions as she shows she is able to be responsible for them. When she fails—and she will—she and her parents discuss the failure, take appropriate action, and then move forward again in the emancipation process. Then her self-esteem will grow by leaps and bounds, and she will feel more confident as she goes through life knowing she can be grateful for her successes, and learn from her failures.

PART V

How Do I Handle My Teenager?

18

THE ADOLESCENT'S SEARCH
FOR SELF-ESTEEM

At last the big day arrives in Jonathon's life. All the years of training, all the years of learning responsibility, all the years of receiving positive feedback from parents are now coming together for the big test: adolescence.

At age nine and ten, Jonathon thought he had a handle on who he was. But now the ground rules are changing almost overnight. His body goes through a metamorphosis, and he goes from being a short fat guy to a tall, thin, lanky young man. He develops a complex skin "disease." Parts of his body erupt with little hairs while other parts of his body explode with pimples. Jonathon becomes so self-conscious about these "physical disorders" that he goes into self-imposed exile so as not to pass on this adolescent "disease" to other family members. Instead of a leper colony, he searches out a teen colony. At this stage, misery loves company.

For the first time, Jonathon wants to talk to girls. He spends hours rehearsing just the right line in front of his mirror, something complicated, such as, "Hi, how are you?"

Then Jonathon finally has the opportunity. He sees *her* in the hall at school. At the perfect moment, when they pass each other and their eyes meet, Jonathon speaks. And out comes a high-pitched squeak. His attempt to say, "Hi, how are you?" with the resonance of a cool baritone comes out sounding like a baby chick running toward its mother.

As humorous as this may sound to adults, the emotional pain of adolescence is excruciating. The isolation is incredible. Teenagers often wonder if they are the only ones on earth being forced to endure all these difficulties. Communication during this period becomes very strained. If Jonathon were able to express his heartfelt thoughts, he might say, "What's wrong with me? I feel so alone."

In a desperate quest to find acceptance, Jonathon tries to look like everyone else his age. Suddenly clothes become very important to him. He might not feel like he's worth much, but the "cool" shirt and name-brand tennis shoes help cover all his erupting flaws.

The first decade of Jonathon's life should have been spent preparing his self-esteem for the world outside the family, where it would receive lots of harsh punches and kicks. Though his self-esteem may have suffered somewhat as a child, adolescence with its freedoms and biological changes will test his maturing self-esteem to its limits.

Where Did My Support Go?

When Jonathon was a child, three institutions should have been helping him build his self-esteem: the family, the school, and the church. These institutions are still available to him, but he does not seem to find as much security from them as he did in the past.

The Family

"I don't fit into my family like I used to," twelve-year-old Richard lamented. "It seems like last year I was like my little brother, a cute little fat guy nobody expects too much from. But now my family expects so much of me. When my dad let me mow the lawn for the first time, I was all excited. But when I tried to start the mower, I pulled the cord so hard I ripped it right off the machine. Boy, was my dad angry."

When adolescents begin to feel more and more awkward about themselves and about their role in the family, they begin to withdraw. Parents, in turn, begin to withdraw as well, thinking their child needs more space or independence. But adolescents also desperately need parental support. They have grown used to their parents being their number-one fans, and they still need parents who applaud and encourage them. If their parents abdicate the "bleacher seats" of encouragement, it will not take long for them to play for just the cheers of peers. Parents must not give up these seats of encouragement and listening.

This is a time, however, when adolescents appear not to want their parents' approval, and indeed, act as if they will have little or nothing to do with their family. Asked to go on a family picnic, the adolescent will probably reply, "Do I have to go?"

In my opinion, adolescents should be required to take part in some of the family's activities. Teens may not know it, but they are desperate to be a part of the family even when they seem to be trying to get out of it. Of course, parents who require their adolescents to attend family functions cannot also require them to act as if they are having a good time. Teenagers will sigh, moan, and groan. They will slouch around and act bored. But the wise parent will do everything possible to include teenagers in the planning process, always realizing that their teenager may not be secure enough to say or act as if they had fun.

When I was twelve and my brother was seven, my family spent three weeks driving from New York to Colorado and back, without air conditioning. Years later, my brother Steve and I, both in our thirties, had lunch with our father and started talking about how much fun we had had on that trip. Right in the middle of our conversation our father interrupted.

"Wait a minute," he broke in. "You two have got to be kidding! All you guys did for three solid weeks was complain. Steve, all I heard you say from the backseat of the car was 'Bobby won't get off of my side. He's squashing me.' Bob, all that came from your mouth was two words, 'I'm bored.' Now, twenty years later, you're trying to say that you had a good time? Are you serious?"

No offense to my father, but what did he expect us to say at that age? "Dad, I want to take this opportunity to tell you how much I appreciate all that you are doing for my personal development. That trip we just went on was a great step forward in my emotional and social development. Thank you for taking me along." Of course not. Parents shouldn't expect their children—especially their insecure adolescent children—to encourage them and thank them.

Putting all of these ingredients together—the fact that teenagers are changing so drastically, feel like they are incapable of doing anything adequately, and are negative about many family experiences—makes it very difficult for them to come to their parents with questions about their physical and emotional development. They desperately need to talk, but many things close off communication, further adding to their feelings of loneliness and isolation.

In some cases, teenagers may think they are bad for the family when their steps toward independence begin to cause family disputes. Teenagers, overhearing their parents argue about rules and behavior, may feel that they are the cause of their parents' problems. They might think, "What a loser I am! Now I'm even making my parents fight."

Teenagers do need to go through a process of emancipation from their family, but they shouldn't separate themselves because they feel too inadequate and unloved to belong to their family. Rather, they should feel free to test their independence, knowing that whatever should happen, they are loved unconditionally and will always be welcomed back into the family.

The School

In fifth grade, Susan loved her teacher. She seemed to be learning well and enjoying her classmates. But when she began middle school that all changed. Now she hates most of her teachers, and she thinks all her classmates are stuck up and boring. What happened?

School is the second institution that has an impact on the needs of children. However, just as the onslaught of puberty has affected Susan's relationship at home, it will also impact her life at school.

Many factors seem to work against Susan's adjustment at school. She is not communicating well with her parents, so she really needs another significant adult in her life, for instance, a teacher. But at her new school she has a different teacher for each class. Because of the system she is not able to develop a warm and intimate relationship with one teacher, and her feelings of isolation increase.

Another factor is the rebellious attitude Susan senses in her new school. Students mouth off at the teachers. They deliberately disobey rules. They cheat and lie. No one seems to be in control, and this frightens her.

Susan also faces intense peer pressure for the first time. She has to decide whether to do what her parents have taught her, or to do what the crowd demands.

Finally, Susan has her own physical changes to deal with. Every time she goes to phys ed class, she is reminded that her body is changing, that she doesn't look as developed as someone else.

I remember well what that first day of phys ed class in middle school. I walked into the locker room and a man handed each of us a towel. "What's this for?" I wondered, looking at it. Then I saw the showers. And my first thought was, "You're kidding! We're all taking a shower after this class—together?"

I looked around me wildly. There was no place to hide. We didn't even get our own room for changing into our gym clothes.

Then I opened my gym bag to find a little box my dad had silently slipped in, with no explanation or instruction. The box said "athletic supporter." As I took it out, I remember thinking, "What is this thing? Do I wear it on my head or what?" What a day that was!

Physical insecurities, peer pressure, negative attitudes at school, and lack of a listening ear are just a few of the pressures teenagers deal with at school. The institution of the school can pose a most vicious attack on the self-esteem of the adolescent. Rather than being an institution that equips and enhances their development, it becomes a fighting arena where their self-esteem is knocked around.

The Church

"What's happened to my child? He used to love Sunday school, and now he acts like he hates it."

Many early adolescents dislike Sunday school. If they are unhappy with school, they are almost surely going to be unhappy about a less familiar environment such as Sunday school. They will say almost anything to get out of going: "The teacher is boring," "All the other kids are weird!" or "Nobody likes me there."

While some churches do not try to reach their teenagers, many do try. So when teenagers blame the church, often they are merely reflecting the way they feel about themselves. They want to enjoy church, but because of their fears of being inadequate, they withdraw, thinking up excuses like "I don't like it when they make me read aloud in class." As ridiculous as that sounds, teenagers are often reluctant to put themselves in a situation where they may once again show the world how inadequate they are. (I guess that doesn't sound so ridiculous. I know some adult men who have those same fears.) Once again, an institution that used to help enhance a child's self-esteem is now a threatening place—all because the child has become an insecure teenager.

Wise parents will do everything possible to help their teenagers deal with Sunday school. If the teenager is afraid she'll look stupid in class, parents could go over next week's Sunday school lesson with her. A few minutes' preparation will help her feel more confident, able to ask and answer questions in class.

Also, parents should be sure to get their children to Sunday school on time or early. If a child is becoming very self-conscious about his body, it can be tremendously embarrassing to walk into class late, with all eyes staring at him.

Parents should try to get involved in the Sunday school experience of the child so that they can know how to make it as comfortable and beneficial as possible for the child. This must be done, however, without getting so involved that the teenager cannot get away from Mom or Dad.

Family, school, and church play major roles in the development of a child's self-esteem. For ten years, children have turned to these institutions for encouragement. Now as teenagers they turn their back on these nurturing institutions, not because they want to, but because they feel unworthy of their nurturing. Alienated and insecure, wanting to feel valuable and belong, they become highly vulnerable, open for the first time to the suggestions of the world.

19

ATTACKED WHILE SELF-ESTEEM IS DOWN

Anyone who has ever played on an athletic team knows the importance of being aware of the strategy and skills of the opponent. In high school, for example, I often spent lunch hours looking at films of the team we would be playing the following Saturday. We needed to be familiar with the enemy so as not to be caught totally unaware.

It is even more important to be prepared for the game of life. Each of us has an enemy to face, and to familiarize us with the enemy's game plan, God has made the "films" of the enemy available for us in the Bible. There we learn of three primary areas that the enemy attacks.

This vivid verbal picture of the enemy's game plan is found in Luke 4:1–12:

> Jesus, full of the Holy Spirit, returned from the Jordan and was led by the Spirit in the desert, where for forty days he was tempted by the devil. He ate nothing during those days, and at the end of them he was hungry. The devil said to him, "If you are the Son of God, tell this stone to become bread." Jesus answered, "It is written: 'Man does not live on bread alone.'" The devil led him up to a high place and showed him in an instant all the kingdoms of the world. And he said to him, "I will give you all their authority and splendor, for it has been given to me, and I can give it to anyone I want to. So if you worship me, it will all be yours." Jesus answered, "It is written: 'Worship the Lord your God and serve him only.'" The devil led him to

Jerusalem and had him stand on the highest point of the temple. "If you are the Son of God," he said, "throw yourself down from here. For it is written: 'He will command his angels concerning you to guard you carefully; they will lift you up in their hands, so that you will not strike your foot against a stone.'" Jesus answered, "It says, 'Do not put the Lord your God to the test.'"

In an attack, place and timing is all-important. Satan always attacks us where we are weakest. Just as in football, where the opponent runs his plays at the parts of the line that are the weakest, so does Satan attack us at our weak points. He also chooses a time when he knows we will be down. In this instance, Satan chose to tempt Christ when he was fasting in a lonely, barren desert.

In this passage, Satan strikes at the heart of three major temptations all humanity must face: physical, social, and intellectual temptation.

First he attacked the physical. "You've fasted long enough," Satan hissed into Jesus' ear. "Why don't you stop this nonsense and eat something? You know you are hungry, so just turn this stone into food."

Then he tried to appeal to Christ's social self. Indicating the world with a sweep of his hand, he said, "Do you see all of the things of this world, Jesus? Everyone will like you if you have them all. And you don't have to wait! They can all be yours if you just bow down and worship me."

Finally, he attacked Christ's intellect. Seeing that Jesus responded to his other two attacks by quoting the Bible, he tried to confuse him by quoting a verse out of context. "You want to throw Bible verses at me, eh, Jesus? Well, how about this one. The Bible says that God will send his angels to guard you. So why not jump off this building? Come on—jump. If you really are the Son of God, you won't be hurt."

This same game plan was used in the Garden of Eden. Satan convinced Eve that the fruit would be three things: good to eat, pleasing to the eye, and able to make her wise (Gen. 3:6). Once again, he tempted her with physical, social, and intellectual temptations.

Satan is still using his three-part strategy today; and why not, if it works? He strikes at us *when* we're weakest; for many people, that time is adolescence. And he strikes *where* we are weakest: again, in the physical, social, and intellectual realms.

Let's take a look at how Satan attacks adolescents in these three areas.

The Physical Battles

Adolescence is largely a twentieth-century phenomenon. In centuries past the young person went through puberty at eleven or twelve and was shortly thereafter considered an adult. In the Jewish culture a boy had a barmitzvah and a girl had a similar ceremony. Other cultures had their rite of passage into adulthood at about the same age, and the child married shortly afterwards. In other words, children went into puberty and only had to deal with their potentially active sex drive for a couple of years.

Today, however, due to nutritional advances, young people are entering puberty at earlier ages, even nine and ten years of age. The average person in America marries in their early to mid-twenties. This means that today's young people must deal with their sex drive, not for two or three years as in the past, but for ten to fifteen years.

The physical temptations of adolescence are obvious. For the first time, teenagers encounter sexual temptations. Even if their parents teach them that sex should wait until marriage, the world works hard to confuse them. One young boy, committed to his faith in Christ, summed up the confusion of his peers very succinctly: "Look, we get sex thrown in our faces all the time. Girls dress in tight clothes to show off their bodies, and almost every movie you see has sex in it. So many kids talk about sex that I began to wonder whether I was the only virgin left in the whole student body."

This student's confession is not out of the ordinary. Teenagers are bombarded with sexual images and sexual connotations. Television makes light of premarital sex, and sitcoms convey the message that the world expects "mature" people to try out their sexuality. That warped message is duplicated by movies, music, and magazines. No wonder there's such an epidemic of teenage pregnancies in America.

Society's misguided attempts to handle this sad state of affairs has played right into the hands of the Enemy. Teaching sexual responsibility today means telling children about contraceptives and abortions. They are told nothing about the beauty of remaining sexually pure. Instead, the underlying message to teenagers is: "Here are the ways to be sexually active without getting caught by a pregnancy: contraceptives and abortions."

Children who have not been trained in God's moral standard for their bodies are bound to give in to this temptation. In the words of one young boy, "God has given me this new body. So why not use it?" Another boy said, "My parents say no just because they don't want me to know how great it is."

The timing for this attack is perfect. With self-esteem at its lowest point, teenagers often feel alienated from the world and their family. They then turn to a sexual partner for companionship and to boost their self-esteem. An attack of this physical temptation is very difficult to repel.

Still, it sometimes amazes me that teenagers can be so lonely that they would risk being sexually active. Even the devastating effects of AIDS seem to have had little effect on many young people. They are still looking to belong to someone regardless of potential consequences.

As if this physical temptation were not enough, there are still further attacks. Often lonely adolescents want to escape—escape their families, escape their school, escape themselves. Now that healthy self-esteem no longer guards them, many teenagers would rather not face the unworthy, unacceptable person they feel they have become. The strong temptation is to escape through substance abuse.

Alcohol and other drugs are another form of physical temptation. "Drugs made me feel good," Billy said, talking about his past problem. "More than that, getting high or drunk helped me forget how inadequate I felt. It got so I felt that I was doing nothing but disappointing my parents. At least when I was high I didn't feel like the loser I had become."

Physical attacks on teenagers are the most obvious. When they were children they may have boldly spoken out against premarital sex and getting high. That, however, was when their self-esteem was strong and their family relationships intact. As teenagers, however, their first line of defense, self-esteem, is down. Feeling unworthy, they are vulnerable to attacks, which come now as never before.

The Social Battle

"I'm so gawky looking, anyway! If I don't give in to sex, or if I don't drink, no one will like me."

Popularity is a very valuable status when one feels unworthy and unlovable. The temptation and ambition to "have it all" no matter what the cost is more than many teenagers can walk away from.

"I knew it was wrong and felt guilty about it," Linda said to her counselor, "but I just wanted friends. I was so lonely that giving in to sex was a way to have people to be with in my new neighborhood." To "be" somebody or to be liked is extremely important when teenagers don't even like themselves very much.

Another major social attack is the temptation of money. This attack, sadly enough, often comes through the father. He'll say, "Son, do you want to be able to live in a house like this? It takes money. That's why you go to school, to get an education so you can make lots of money. If you don't get better grades, you're going to end up as a ditchdigger with nothing to show for it."

How many of us have heard that sermon? It may have worked as a motivator a few generations ago, but not today. Today's child is faced with the tremendous temptation to be somebody, and they know that to be a somebody you have to be rich. Ironically, they used to be a "somebody" when they were just cute helpless children. Now to be somebody they have to have something.

"My dad thinks it takes an education to make money," Linda said. "He's crazy. I can go downtown to sell drugs and make more on a Saturday night than he makes all week." That frightening statement is 100 percent correct. There must be more of a reason to get an education than just to make money. But then, there must be a better way to pursue happiness than to have money.

Teenagers need role models to inspire them, especially at this stage in life when they feel so unworthy. When I was a child with an ambition to be somebody in life, I looked around me for adult role models. (Of course I didn't call them that at the time. I just saw that they were people I admired.) I tried to look beyond my teenage peers and focus on these adults. I knew if I followed their example I had a good chance of becoming a "somebody."

Unfortunately, however, role models for children are scarce. An Italian mother on the block where I grew up used to brag, "This is America. When my son grows up he can be anything. He can even be president!" Parents don't say things like that anymore. The positions that used to receive a great deal of respect are now ridiculed. Some children may grow up never hearing their parents say one positive word about America's highest office.

Ask some teenager what he thinks about pursuing some of the positions available to him.

ADULT: What do you want to be when you grow up? What are your ambitions?

TOM: I don't know.

ADULT: How about a medical doctor?

TOM: Nah, my parents say they're only interested in getting your money and don't really care about making people well.

ADULT: What about studying to be a lawyer?

TOM: No, my dad says they're in it for the power and the money. They don't really care about the law.

ADULT: Oh, well, what about becoming a teacher?

TOM: Dad says teachers are people who can't get jobs anyplace else. They don't care about kids. They just want to strike every year.

ADULT: Did you ever think about sticking with basketball and becoming a professional athlete?

TOM: What's so good about those guys? My dad showed me an article in a sports magazine that showed that 85 percent of all pro basketball players take drugs.

ADULT: (feeling desperate) What about becoming a utility worker?

TOM: What do they do? My dad always points them out to me parked alongside the road taking a coffee break. He says they are all lazy.

ADULT: (with only one last hope) What about becoming a pastor?

TOM: That's the *last* thing I'd want to be. My dad says all pastors do is make people feel guilty and ask for more money.

This boy would love to have a role model to look up to and to emulate. Unfortunately, his parents have successfully pointed out the bad apples in each profession. Where are the role models for today's youth to look up to? In its quest for power and money, our society has destroyed them.

With such a picture of society painted for teenagers, why should they try to play by the rules? When they see and hear only about the failures in each profession, they will have no desire to study and work hard. Or worse, they will adopt the warped motives of society, studying and working hard only in hopes of making money and wielding power.

Many young people today are drifting aimlessly because they have no goals. One year several college students stayed with us during their spring break, and I asked one of the boys what he wanted to do after he finished school. He did not have any idea, nor was he sure he liked the course of study he was taking. Finally he admitted, "I would like to be able to pick a profession that I feel my parents would be proud of, something I could go home and tell them about and they would just smile. But my dad thinks everybody with an education is dishonest and wasting their time. When I tell him how wonderful Dr. Parker at school has been, my dad just cuts him down. Sometimes I feel it would be easier flipping hamburgers."

This boy's father obviously had his own set of problems. He was paying for his son's education, so he obviously did not believe all the negatives that he had showered on his son. However, his son did not seem to know that. He was not secure enough to see his dad's own insecurities or problems.

This young man looked to his parents for approval, but when he presented them with possible goals he could pursue or role models he respected, his dad burst all his balloons, leaving him without direction, goals, or motivation. Unaware of the impact they had on his self-esteem, his parents pulled their encouragement out from under him, and his self-esteem dropped. How much better for him if they had realized he needed their support socially in order to avoid the temptations of money and power.

The Intellectual Battle

Walking out of church on Sunday morning, the Anderson family was all smiles. The pastor's sermon was about loving your neighbor, and Mr. and Mrs. Anderson said wonderful things to everyone they passed between the pew and the car. The Anderson children, Rick and Amanda, watched as their parents modeled true Christian graciousness.

But when the family got into the car and closed the

doors, the adult conversation took a major turn. "Could you believe that he preached that message again?" Mr. Anderson said to his wife. "And he went over twelve o'clock, as well."

"What I could not believe," Mrs. Anderson joined in, "was that ridiculous hat Erma Flatrock had on."

Rick and Amanda, sitting in the back seat listening, learn quickly that the Christian walk is just for church—not for the rest of the time. They've just had their first lesson in adult hypocrisy.

Children tend to believe whatever their parents tell them. When children enter adolescence, however, they begin to scrutinize the world. Feeling shaky about who they are and where they belong, they look for flaws or hypocrisies in their parents. They do not really want to find flaws, for their parents are their source of strength. But if they discover that their parents are hypocrites, they don't really feel compelled to follow their leadership. So they look elsewhere.

Even parents who try to live consistently are fallible. However, parents who do not try to set an example for their children destroy the foundation of strength for which insecure adolescents are searching. All of this makes them very vulnerable to a world that is constantly challenging their beliefs.

When the teacher notified Mr. Anderson that Rick had been caught cheating on a test, Mr. Anderson decided to have a talk with Rick on the importance of being honest and obeying rules. So they got into the car to go for a drive, and Mr. Anderson began his sermon on the importance of obeying the rules.

Finally Rick interrupted, "But Dad, I only looked on the other paper because the teacher didn't give us enough time to study for the test."

"It doesn't matter, son," Mr. Anderson replied. "It's against the rules to look at another student's paper, and we must all obey the rules whether we agree with them or not." A piercing beep interrupted him. "There's the fuzz buster. I better slow down."

This parent was completely unaware of the double message he was sending his son, lecturing him on honesty while he used a device to evade the law. In other words, being able to speed was more important to him than the moral development of his son.

Children collect these more obvious hypocrisies and become easy targets for intellectual temptations. They learn that it is not important to be honest, even though their parents tell them that it is. What is most important in life is not doing what's right, but not getting caught when you do something wrong. Parents who do not walk the Christian talk teach their children a sad lesson.

I went to college with a boy whose dad was a pastor. I had just become a Christian, so I was asking him some questions. Finally he said to me, "The Christian life is a farce, so why try it? I ought to know. I grew up in church."

What a responsibility parents have to equip their children for battle against the temptations of life! The greatest way parents can help is to be the role model the child needs. They must do what they tell their children to do, and when they make a mistake they must be willing to admit it.

Teenagers are vulnerable and often feel desperate in their battle with the world. With their self-esteem temporarily shattered, they need to be able to find strength, consistent leadership, and love in their family. The family's consistent life may be just the strength they can fall back on when dealing with temptations.

I remember watching those films of the team we would

be facing on the following Saturday. I remember thinking, *Those guys are going to kill us!* We generally did very well against our opponents, however. Our coach spent a lot of time preparing us for the game, and then, when we were on our own on the field, he was always available on the sidelines for consultation and encouragement. As bad as the bumps and bruises were, we usually won because we had been prepared. Preparation and encouragement are winning ingredients.

20

ADOLESCENCE: SOME FINAL THOUGHTS

"It's just amazing what a child has to live with today, especially if you live in a metropolitan area as I do," one parent said to me. "As soon as we get the chance, we are going to relocate and raise our children in a rural mountain atmosphere. That way we won't have to deal with the problems we're facing now."

Many parents today have adopted this philosophy of "it will all be OK when we move out into the country." I now live in southern Florida. Down here, people talk about the mountains of North Carolina. They say they want to move to the Smoky Mountains so that their children will not be faced with the temptations they face in Florida.

Personally, I find humor in parental quests to help children by isolating them. In 1966, I left the suburbs of New York City and Washington, D.C. to go to college in the Smoky Mountains of eastern Tennessee. I shared an apartment there with a high-school football coach. He used to tell me hair-raising stories about the drug abuse and other problems in the local schools.

"What are they doing to fight the problem?" I asked.

"Fight the problem! They won't even admit that we have a problem!" he said. "I have continually brought it up and they continually indicate that that is a topic they don't want discussed."

There is no escaping problems. Suburban New York and

rural Tennessee both had the same difficulties. The only difference seemed to be that the big cities tried to do something to help the young people. Unfortunately, many rural adults in decision-making positions back then simply hid their heads in the sand and denied that a problem existed.

It does not matter where we live with our children. What matters most is what we parents do with the children God has given to us. Families should not move from place to place to shield children from the temptations of the world. Rather, parents should train their children in such a consistent manner that they have confidence wherever they go.

Relocating the family to help children may actually have just the opposite effect on them. Many boys who come to Sheridan House, for example, are there because of problems brought on by a move. Parents will bring their son to us and say, "I don't know what happened to Kyle. He was doing fine in school and at home until last year."

I then ask, "Did anything of note happen to your family to cause his change in behavior?"

"Well, yes," they reply, "we moved out of a bad neighborhood into a new home in a beautiful location. But that should have helped Kyle, shouldn't it?"

"You would think that that would be an asset," I say. "But did any other change accompany this move?"

"Well, yes, we both had to go to work for the first time, to be able to afford our new home."

This move caused two dramatic changes in this child's life: loss of a parent at home and loss of a familiar neighborhood. Obviously, Kyle did not need a new house as much as he needed a parent's input. Moving was traumatic for him because he had known in his old neighborhood how he fit into his environment and who he was in relation to the various neighbors who have watched him grow.

Anyone who has gone back to the home of his childhood knows the wonderful and secure feeling one gets from seeing the neighborhood he grew up in. In contrast, moving to a new neighborhood forces a child to start finding out all over again who he is and how he fits in.

Whether you can stay in one place or are forced into moving, the key is to invest in the child. Give her the necessary training and love and don't stop, even when she may act indifferent.

Preparing for the Blows

In high school I was a wide receiver on the football team. My coach made us spend what seemed to be an incredible amount of time working on grueling neck exercises. I complained and did everything I could to get out of these neck workouts. They made absolutely no sense to me. When I asked him why we did them, his reply didn't convince me that the pain of the exercises was worth it. But the coach made me do them anyway.

Then came the first game. In the second quarter I went out for a pass. It was thrown so high that I had to jump to catch it. Just then, the defender tackled me at my ankles. I did a complete flip and landed on the back of my neck. A hush fell over the stadium. The audience thought I had broken my neck. But I jumped up and ran back to the huddle ready for the next play. I felt no pain.

Later on as I saw the film of that particular play and realized how serious that blow could have been, I looked back at the coach and he just smiled and winked. His training program had saved me from being hurt by the tremendous blow I had received. He did not save me from the blow. But he did spend hours preparing me for it.

I cannot save my child from the blows and temptations of life, even though, as a parent, I would like to. Instead, I must prepare my child to face life in such a way as to help him get back up after he has been knocked down. Not because the child says, "Train me." No—I do it simply because it is my job as a parent to do so.

We cannot always shield our children from life's difficulties and temptations. Someday they will leave home and be forced to deal with what the world has to throw at them. The teenage years are the practice years. Adolescence is a time when they go out into the world and hear, feel, and even experience what is out there. But they also come home to their parents each night. The wise parent is more than available to listen to the teenager and discuss what is out there.

Cloaked Communication

The caring parent will also be available at all times to listen to what her child is asking. Quite often the adolescent is not completely sure how to phrase the important questions on his mind. Some questions may come at inopportune moments or the questions may be well disguised. Therefore parents should always be alert to any signal their children may be sending them.

In the book *Signals*, Paul Ackerman and Murray Kappelman tell the story of Debbie. When Debbie turned eleven her parents sat her down and talked with her about her sexual development. They explained a woman's menstrual cycle and how it played a part in childbirth. Months later, Debbie had her first period. A few months later, as is often the case with young girls going through adolescence, she missed one of her periods.

One evening as her mother was finishing up the dishes, Debbie walked in and very offhandedly asked, "Didn't you tell me, Mom, that one way a woman knows that she is going to have a baby is when she skips her period?"

Without even turning around to look at her daughter, her mother answered, "Yes, honey, that's correct."

The mother went back to her chores, and Debbie went back to her room to meditate on what she feared had happened to her. Though she had not had sex, she felt that somehow she had gotten pregnant.

Quite by chance, Debbie's mother was walking by the bathroom later that night and casually pushed open the partially closed door. There to her horror she found Debbie, about to swallow a bottle of pills. She learned the hard way that parents need to listen to what the child is *really* communicating behind the words.

When a child refuses to communicate, one way I encourage them to talk is to listen to tapes with them. If something of interest is mentioned on the tape, parent or child can stop the tape and discuss what they just heard. It is easier to talk about certain topics in such an instance because someone else, rather than parent or child, has brought up the topic. Parents should remember, however, that the teenager may give little or no indication that the listening experience was beneficial or enjoyable. Yet the parent should do it anyway, in as pleasurable and unintimidating an atmosphere as possible.

A Winning Team

As I mentioned earlier in the book, children need to feel like they are an essential part of a special team. The same is true for adolescents. They must see themselves as belonging to a "winning team," a family that works and plays together. Parents should keep working on family tradition and should keep having fun so that teenagers can fall back on their family's healthy attitudes. This kind of family strength will help teenagers weather the storms of negative feelings they may have.

Vince Lombardi, the famous football coach, was renowned for shaping college players into winning teams. When he first arrived at Green Bay, Wisconsin, to take on his new position as coach for the Packers, he had some good players recruited from college teams. For some reason, however, these players were acting like a ragtag bunch of losers.

Coach Lombardi had other ideas. He intended to whip them into shape as a team, to make them proud of themselves and of their team. Through structure, discipline, and extra attention, Lombardi was able to change this losing team into the best in the National Football League. As the players began to feel better about the team they belonged to, they in turn felt like they themselves were more valuable.

Many of those players from the original Lombardi Green Bay team have gone on to be very successful in other endeavors, such as business. Even now, decades later, some of them have pictures of Coach Lombardi hanging in their offices. When they were interviewed for a documentary on their former coach, one player after another attributed Lombardi's constant positive attitude toward the team and each individual player as a major reason for their success. This father figure, now deceased, believed in them when they were at the lowest point in their careers. And his attitude made them believe in themselves.

The parallel is obvious. When teenagers feel incompetent and ugly, the parents as their coaches must act as if they are still valuable, making them a vital part of family activities. Often at this time of life, who they belong to may be all that matters to a teenager. When they are disappointed with who they are, their only salvation lies in who or what they belong to.

EPILOGUE

When I was three years old I spent a week with an aunt. One evening when it was time for my bath she took me into the bathroom. She had started to undress me when I abruptly stopped her. With as much of an indignant attitude as a three-year-old can muster, I announced that I would not undress in front of her. So my elderly aunt left the bathroom, and I undressed myself in private. Then, naked, I flung open the bathroom door, walked out in the hall, and told my aunt that she could come in now.

At three years old, I knew that there was supposed to be something private about nakedness. I was just not quite sure what it was. Years later, however, I was made "naked" in a more revealing way.

As a junior in college I appeared to have it made. I was an officer in my fraternity, I played college sports, and socially I was at the hub of activities. I was trying very hard to be somebody. At this time, I began dating a girl who was very different from me. She was from a missionary family. She was not an officer in a sorority, an athlete, or a cheerleader, and she did not chase after dates like many of the other girls on campus. This young freshman coed named Rosemary could have belonged to any organization she chose. Instead, she chose to be active in church and spend time in wholesome activities with her friends.

Rosemary had one other thing: a very strong self-esteem. She obviously knew who she was and whose she was. Her sweet confidence totally baffled me. She maintained a solid consistency. I, on the other hand, vacillated dramatically according to how my various activities were lifting me up.

In order to date Rosemary on Saturday night I had to go to church on Sunday with her. Initially I asked her out for Friday nights to avoid the church obligation. As I got more and more interested in her, however, I became reluctant to let any of the other anxious suitors have an opportunity. I soon stopped leaving her Saturday nights available for other guys.

Over the months, Rosemary could hardly keep quiet about the relationship she had with Jesus Christ. She talked about how he loved her completely even though she claimed to be so unworthy.

In going to church with Rosemary, I soon became acquainted with her pastor. The Reverend Spurgeon McCart was a thick-handed, strong-looking man who exuded the same confidence about his relationship with Christ as Rosemary did. It was not long before he, too, was talking to me about my need for Christ. I listened politely but thought to myself that I just did not belong in this kind of religious world.

A few months later my self-image began to crumble. I saw that I would never be good enough to play first string in college sports. If I had been asked in high school to define who I was, I would certainly have started with the label of athlete. Now to be forced to admit to myself that I really was not good enough for college sports was devastating. I was no longer an athlete; I was now a spectator.

I became bitter. My friendships soured, and my grades dropped. With the loss of my athletic identity, I felt as if the real me had been made naked for all the world to see. I no longer could cover myself with the label of athlete. Without having these activities to excel in, who was I? Who could love, or even like, the real naked me now that I could no longer perform? This nakedness became very difficult to live with. I became even more bitter. I felt as though I did not belong anywhere or to anyone.

When my self-esteem had hit rock bottom my college brought in a special speaker, the nation's most prominent atheist—Madalyn Murray O'Hair. As soon as I saw the notices posted for her lectures, I decided to attend. Maybe Mrs. O'Hair would have the real answers for which I was searching so desperately.

I had convinced Rosemary that since I was visiting her church with her, the least she could do was come and hear Madalyn Murray O'Hair with me. When we arrived at the auditorium, it was filling quickly. Soon there was standing room only.

Mrs. O'Hair took the stand. She began to speak. To my shock, vile and incredible bitterness poured out with her every breath. Not only were her words and ideas offensive, but also the way she said them. Uneasy, I glanced around to see how the audience was taking it.

Just then I spotted Rosemary's pastor, Spurgeon McCart. He stood in the back, leaning against the wall. But something seemed strange. I looked again. And then I saw the tears streaming down this strong man's cheeks.

Bewildered, I turned to Rosemary and pointed out her pastor. "Why is he crying?" I whispered. "This lady is cursing everything he believes in. How could that make him cry?"

Rosemary said, "Reverend McCart probably feels sorry for her. What you are witnessing is the true compassion of Christ regardless of behavior or attitude. He feels bad that something has caused her to be so bitter."

Her answer took me aback. All weekend I puzzled over the speech, Reverend McCart's tears, and Rosemary's explanation, until I finally realized that I had found the answer that I had been looking for. I found the one Person who loved me completely and unconditionally. I found the one Person who knew my inner feelings, my nakedness. I found the one Person who could answer the question of who I was. I found Jesus Christ, the Person who loved me so much that he chose to die so that I could spend eternity with him.

I realized that I needed two basic questions answered: Who am I? and Where do I belong? Sure, I eventually wanted the answers to other questions, like what I should do with my life after college, who I should marry, and other questions like that. I knew, however, that these two very basic questions had to be addressed first, or I would just continue to follow the crowd as I made my decisions.

Who was I? I was beginning to see, with the help of Rosemary and the Bible, that I was a child of God. That, in itself, also answered the second question: Where did I belong? I belonged to God. I no longer had to belong to a sports team to feel good about myself. I was a child of the King. I was somebody because of Christ.

Thanks to Madalyn Murray O'Hair, I gave my life to Christ that weekend. It was an uphill battle, but my self-esteem was tremendously impacted as I realized that I did not have to perform to earn God's love. I was adopted into the King's family simply because he loved me, warts and all.

I wrote this book to help parents enhance their child's self-esteem. By making their child a priority, by listening, loving, teaching, and playing with their child, he or she will grow in confidence. The final answer for the self-esteem of a child, teenager, or adult, however, is the love and forgiveness of Jesus Christ. Nothing and nobody else can provide for your children the security, love, and acceptance that a relationship with Christ provides.

One final note: in the summer of 1972, Rosemary agreed to become my wife. And she is still being used by God to enhance my self-esteem.